SOCIAL NETWORKS INFORMAL CARE AND PUBLIC POLICY

Peter Willmott

Research Report 655

Policy Studies Institute

PSI Own Series Reports

Sales Representation: Frances Pinter (Publishers) Ltd.
25 Floral Street
London WC2E 9DS

Orders to: Marston Book Services
P.O. Box 87
Oxford OX4 1LB

ISBN 0-85374-275-8

Published by Policy Studies Institute
100 Park Village East, London NW1 3SR
Printed by Bourne Offset Ltd.

CONTENTS

Contents

ACKNOWLEDGEMENTS

The research was funded by the Economic and Social Research Council (Award no. G00232132). It forms part of a wider programme of work which is supported by the Joseph Rowntree Memorial Trust. Help with special analyses was given by Ian Cullen of the Bartlett School of Architecture and Planning, University College London. Michael Bayley, David Challis, Roger Hadley and Stephen Hatch commented on the final chapter, and my PSI colleagues Isobel Allen and Donald Derx on the draft as a whole. Particular thanks are due to Martin Bulmer, Peter Marris and Phyllis Willmott, who in commenting on the draft suggested many useful amendments and additions.

I INTRODUCTION

Personal relationships with friends, relatives, neighbours and work colleagues are crucial in every society. Though largely hidden beneath the large and visible institutions that so obviously influence people's opportunities and daily lives, this subterranean informal order is important for many reasons. Along with the nuclear family, which is at its core, it has the responsibility for 'socialisation' - for imbuing infants with the values, rules and customs of their culture. It forms an essential set of 'mediating structures' which 'stand between the individual in his private sphere and the large institutions of the public sphere' (Berger, 1977). It accounts for most of the sociable human contact which people apparently need and enjoy. And it is a major source of support and practical help.

Because of this last function in particular (though not only because of that) informal social relationships are relevant to policy. In a period when there is likely to be growing pressure on public spending, it makes sense to understand more clearly the help and support that people give each other informally. To do so should help in the formulation of policy, since there is - and is likely to be under any future British government whatever its political complexion - increasing emphasis on the contribution of the informal sector and on the ways in which it could be strengthened by statutory support.

The main aim of this report is, therefore, to examine patterns of personal relationships in present-day Britain, with a particular eye to their relevance for policy. The central policy interest is in the contribution of informal care, but policies for housing and town planning, among others, also have a bearing on companionship and informal care because of their capacity to sustain or weaken existing social patterns and encourage or discourage the development of new ones.

1

The place of social theory

Although policy is the main concern, it is not the only one. Thinking about policy will be more useful if it is based on a better understanding than we now have of what is happening, and that requires not just reporting the facts but explaining them, or at least trying to do so. This is, or ought to be, the function of social theory.

The best-known interpretations of informal relationships so far offered by sociologists have been in terms of long-term historical trends. The 'founding fathers' of sociology, and others after them, were concerned - 'obsessed' would hardly be too strong a word - with the ways in which industrialisation and urbanisation were transforming social relationships. Most of these men were essentially conservative in outlook, believing that trends in society after the Industrial Revolution, whatever gains they might be bringing, were at the same time breaking up the traditional social bonds and replacing them with anomie and alienation. Comte, for instance, worried over the breakdown of traditional forms of association and lamented 'the anarchy which day by day envelops society' (quoted in Nisbet, 1967). Simmel, in a characteristic passage, said of modern urban life: 'We frequently do not even know by sight those who have been our neighbours for years' (Simmel, 1905). Wirth (1938) said that social relationships in modern cities were 'impersonal, superficial, transitory and segmental'. The anxiety about the trends was often expressed by the early sociologists in the form of a simple two-fold model: the past represented human warmth and solidarity, the future anonymity and isolation. The best-known of these dichotomies comes from the German sociologist Tönnies (1887), who distinguished between Gemeinschaft and Gesellschaft and saw an irreversible historical shift from the communal attachments of the first (whose 'three pillars' he described as kinship, neighbourhood and friendship) to the less binding associational patterns of the second.

Other sociologists took a less simplified view, arguing that though the forms of the social bond might change there would continue to be close personal relationships. Durkheim (1893), for instance, believed that new forms of social solidarity, based on people's occupations, would take the place of the old. Weber (1922) argued that Tönnies's two kinds of relationship were not mutually exclusive, but that either could be transformed into the other; thus friends might become business associates or, conversely, business associates become personal friends. And some of Wirth's colleagues in the famous Chicago school of sociology took a much less gloomy view than he did of relationships in the modern city.

2

Research in the past forty years, in North America as well as Britain, has lent more support to the second body of sociological opinion than the first, and many of the findings from those studies are cited in subsequent chapters. The main point to be underlined is that, although human society has clearly changed dramatically, the consequence has manifestly not been a simple one-way process from solidarity to impersonality.

Problems of language

The task of analysing informal relationships is complicated by conceptual and terminological difficulties. The word community, applied increasingly in an ever-widening range of ways, is an obvious example, but even such everyday terms as friend and neighbour pose problems. Most of the terms to do with relationships, groups and communities are taken up later in successive chapters, but some definitions need to be dealt with at the outset.

The first is the term social network. The expression is currently used, by both professional social researchers and non-specialists, in two senses. In the most limited one it simply refers to the various people that a particular person knows: we can broadly describe that set of people as his or her network, whether the other members of the network know each other or not. This is the definition adopted in a number of recent studies of informal care, including those by Sinclair et al. (1984) and Wenger (1984). In the second usage, the one more usually employed by students of social networks, the notion is applied more fully. Barnes first introduced it in an influential article in 1954:

> Each person is, as it were, in touch with a number of people, some of whom are directly in touch with each other and some of whom are not ... I find it convenient to talk of a social field of this kind as a network. The image I have is of a number of points, some of which are joined by links.

The idea has since been taken up by others. Among them, Bott (1957) drew a useful distinction between social networks which were 'loose-knit' and those which were 'close-knit', a concept which has subsequently been expressed in terms of 'density', a relatively dense network being a close-knit one - one in which a large proportion of the possible links between people exists in practice.

The idea of networks in this fuller sense has not only been widely adopted by social scientists (for example, Mitchell, 1969; Boissevain, 1974; Fischer et al., 1977; Fischer, 1982). Along with

3

the more limited meaning, it has entered general usage. This is no doubt because for most people it indicates what they recognise as the reality of contemporary social relationships. All of one's acquaintances, friends and relatives do not know each other but some do, and those who do can be seen as linked with each other in one network or another. There is a contrast here with simpler societies and earlier times, in which most people in a particular group, especially in a particular locality, know - or knew - each other and few outsiders.

The other semantic issues to be briefly considered here are to do with the language of care. The key terms that need to be clarified, by way of background, are community care, social care and informal care.

The gap between the official term and what is actually happening is probably greater in connection with community care than any other field of social policy (Walker, 1986). The official policy of community care has gained momentum since it was launched thirty years ago, the reason being at least partly the concern with public spending mentioned earlier. The initial concern, in the late 1950s, was to move mentally ill and mentally handicapped people out of large hospitals and institutions. The aim has subsequently been extended to cover other categories of people such as the elderly and the chronically sick. Policy-makers have meanwhile taken an increasingly broad and diversified view of the resources 'in the community' that might be drawn upon, with the informal contribution taking an ever more central place in official thinking.

A government White Paper on the elderly in 1981 acknowledged that 'the primary sources of support and care of elderly people are informal and voluntary'. The White Paper added that these sources 'spring from the personal ties of kinship, friendship and neighbourhood', and went on to assert, borrowing a distinction initially made by Bayley (1973), that 'Care in the community must increasingly mean 'Care by the community' (Department of Health and Social Security, 1981).

Although there remains a good deal of confusion in official circles, it seems that in terms of government policy community care has now come to mean three different things. One (chronologically the first) meaning - as in the phrase 'care in the community' just quoted - is simply care other than in a hospital or institution. In certain circumstances the Department of Health and Social Security (DHSS) includes as part of community care some local small-scale hospitals or residential homes, drawing the distinction between these and non-local larger ones (DHSS, 1977), but the general idea holds. The second meaning of community care is a more positive version of the first, covering all the care given 'in the community' (that is, other than in a large institution) from the full range of sources including informal. The third meaning, laying the emphasis on care by the community (as in the 1981 White Paper), is confined to the voluntary and informal contributions. This third sense is the most relevant to the present report.

Social care was defined by Philip Abrams (1978) as 'all forms of care and treatment other than medical care and direct cash support'. Such care comes from four main sources: statutory, private, organised voluntary and, of course, informal (Wolfenden Report, 1978). Wolfenden defined informal care in particular as 'the help and support that family, friends and neighbours give to each other'. Gilroy (1982) has distinguished some of the categories of informal care: putting people in touch with the 'formal services'; sharing information or giving advice; providing practical help, through for example a gift or loan, or help with accommodation; providing emotional support, for example with problems of 'isolation or alienation'; providing personal - and sometimes intimate - care of the kind described by Parker (1981) as 'tending' to distinguish it from the broader and vaguer 'caring'. A distinction between the different forms of informal care is taken up more systematically in the final chapter. Meanwhile, a central question, in reviewing the evidence on relationships, is about the availability of informal sources of care.

The boundaries of informal care
Which kinds of carers should be included as informal as distinct from formal? It has to be recognised that, though the difference is real enough, no precise definition can be entirely satisfactory: the boundaries are both open and fluid. But some broad lines can be distinguished.

Statutory and private care and even much voluntary care is obviously formal, not informal. Gilroy (1982) suggested that the following should also be excluded from the informal sector: 'activities undertaken within some external organisation, however loose that may be (for example, mutual aid schemes); voluntary activity in which there is a degree of accountability to an intermediary'. Though this is helpful as a general rule, it cannot be applied too rigidly. First, mutual aid schemes, community groups and the like may be started in a formal or semi-formal way, but some of the members may later come to develop strong informal relationships with each other. The same can be true to some extent of any voluntary (or, for that matter, even paid) activity where there is formal accountability. Philip Abrams found, in studying organised 'neighbourhood care' and similar schemes, that participants in such schemes often developed personal friendships with each other: 'I don't call her "Home Warden" or "Mrs", I call her "Alice"' (Bulmer, 1986). The formal, in other words, was to some extent transformed into the informal - an example of the very process which Weber had described.

Care within the nuclear family is another boundary area. Most of it is part of ordinary life, and the label 'informal care' seems inappropriate for normal everyday caring given by a husband and wife to each other, and by either or both to their children. Sometimes, however, care within the family needs to be so arduous or long-standing that it might reasonably be expected to come, at least in part, from the formal services, and in such cases the carer or carers could be regarded as informal substitutes for - or complements to - formal care. Examples are the care given by parents to a severely handicapped child, or that given by an elderly person to a frail spouse. Though these are discussed in later chapters, normal care within the nuclear family is not considered, and personal relationships within the nuclear family - together with those between cohabitees or lovers - are not covered in this review.

The main focus is on relationships with relatives outside the nuclear family, with friends and with neighbours, all of whom can be seen as potential sources of informal care. Relatives in particular often do help, but they do not have the same statutory responsibility to do so as husbands and wives have for each other and parents have for dependent children. As Firth and his colleagues (1969) have pointed out:

... apart from certain legal obligations regarding 'next of kin', the great body of extra-familial kin are free from any general social formulations about behaviour to relatives... Obligations and responsibilities have to be assessed in the light of personal judgement, not formal rule.

The question of social class
Some clarification is also needed about the concept of social class. Most research studies show differences between the classes in Britain in their patterns of kinship, friendship and neighbouring. This is hardly surprising since social class variations have been observed in respect of many other matters, from infant mortality to housing tenure and from marriage age to leisure patterns (see

for example Reid, 1977 and 1981). But is is worth giving some preliminary attention to the notion, and also to why it is relevant to informal relationships.

First, what social class refers to. Marxists, and some others, define it solely in an economic sense: your class depends upon your relationship to the means of production. But this goes against ordinary usage and, in common with most non-marxist sociologists, I employ the term as a general heading covering a number of personal and family characteristics that tend to go together in all advanced societies: income, ownership of property, family connections, education, occupational status. These are often associated with each other for obvious reasons: a well-educated person is for instance likely to have a professional occupation, some property and a fairly high income; a person with limited skills is likely to have a relatively low-paid job, little property and little in the way of influential family links. But Britain is not a rigid 'caste'-type society; there is a degree of educational and occupational mobility from one generation to the next. For other reasons too the correspondence between the different dimensions is far from absolute: the school teacher may be well-educated but poor, the successful businessman less well-educated but rich. No single index of social position is entirely satisfactory, though some are better than others and a good one is usually adequate when it comes to discussing broad differences in behaviour. Most of the surveys referred to here follow the Registrar General in classifying people on the basis of their occupation.

Why should social class have any bearing on the subject-matter of this study? One reason is to do with opportunities. People with relatively large incomes and with property, and to some extent those with educational qualifications, have more choice about their lives, because they have more resources - material or cultural - at their disposal. They are likely to have more say over where they live, they more often have cars, telephones and spacious homes, and all these can have some bearing on their relationships with others. They are also likely to have more power and are therefore better able to make formal systems of care work for them, to buy care.

Secondly, their attitude to their work is usually different. People with manual jobs, even skilled ones, may get some satisfaction from their work, but they mainly see it as a means of earning a living and, in any event, they seldom have much prospect of advancement up a promotional ladder. Middle-class people - those with professional, managerial or administrative jobs - are on the contrary likely to see their occupation - and to a large extent

7

their whole life - as a career ladder, working and hoping for a progression not only in income (though that is a major difference between the classes) but in power, influence and status. As Michael Young and I found in a study of family life, work and leisure in the London Metropolitan Region (Young and Willmott, 1973) middle-class men's jobs and careers were more often what Dubin (1956) called their 'central life interest' than were those of working-class men. This salience of career in one's life, together with ownership of one's home, makes a middle-class person more likely and more able to move home when a new and better job requires it. And this propensity to move can, in turn, affect the proximity of relatives.

It also affects the capacity to strike up friendly relationships with strangers. When sociologists talk about the 'social skills' of middle-class people compared with working-class, they are not making any general judgement about innate capacities. Social skills are needed among miners working together on a coalface, in a team of dockers or among manual workers who meet regularly in a pub; these skills are, however, different from those that help make friends in a new neighbourhood. The people (mainly middle-class) who have become accustomed to moving their home and district relatively often have had the opportunity to learn how to settle quickly in a strange area, whereas those (in the past mainly working-class people) who have tended to stay put are less likely to have developed the same capacities.

These are by no means the only explanations for the class differences that are so consistently reported in the research. They are examples only but they are enough, I hope, to indicate the relevance of the social class structure. In this report, class differences are mainly discussed in terms of two grouping: the middle-class (broadly people with professional and executive jobs, and the things that usually go with those) and the working class (broadly those with manual or routine non-manual jobs, and the things that usually go with those), though detailed comparisons are sometime drawn. Throughout it should be remembered that the notion is not precise, that the boundaries are blurred and that the terms are being used as a form of shorthand.

As will become apparent, much of the material in this report comes from surveys that are some years old. In addition most of the research is locally-based, so that it is difficult to make assessments about the national picture. These studies provide a guide to what is happening, but the limitations should be borne in mind.

The next chapters look in turn at what is known about relationships with three particular categories of people - relatives, friends and neighbours - and about the care and support which informed networks provide. Under each heading an attempt is made to see which kinds of people, living in which kinds of places, provide and receive more help, and which less.

Chapter V brings the material together so as to identify the distinctive contributions from the different sources, and also examines the informal relationships of various kinds of people who might be judged 'at risk' of lacking companionship and informal support. An across-the-board assessment is made in Chapter VI of the relevance of neighbourhood and community in contemporary Britain. A final chapter suggests some of the implications for policy and research.

II KINSHIP

Though relatives play a larger part in simpler societies than they do in our own, they are of some importance in the lives of most people in Britain, and are the main providers of informal care. Kinship relationships derive from three kinds of link. The first is biological: the 'blood' tie is through descent or common ancestry. The second source is marriage, as a result of which one acquires in-laws. The third bond is a legal one, as in an adoptive relationship.

As the previous chapter suggested, relationships with kin outside the nuclear family are, in advanced societies, very much a matter of personal choice. There are, however, clear patterns in what actually happens.

The nuclear family is itself the key. After children leave their parents to set up an independent home, the generations usually continue to maintain the ties already developed between them. As a result the closest kinship relationships, measured in the frequency of contact and the extent of help, are those between parents and adult children, and to a lesser between brothers and sisters sharing the same parents. Every wedding links two existing families through the newly-created one, and after marriage a person's parents-in-law and brothers and sisters-in-law also became important. Other relationships draw such strengths as they have from these. Because parents, when they have children of their own, normally continue to maintain contact with their parents, there is usually contact, often close, between grandparents and grandchildren, and most people - particularly as children - also meet their uncles, aunts and cousins through their parents' continuing contacts with their siblings. In British, as in other western societies, more distant relatives than these seldom figure much in people's lives unless they happen to live nearby and often not even then.

In describing kinship, a crucial distinction is that between the perspective of younger people and that of the older generation. If, for instance, one asks younger adults how often they see their parents, the answers are likely to be different from those given by older people when asked about contacts with the child they see most: most parents see one of their children more often than others, and it follows that other children see their parents less. Furthermore, the needs of elderly people, particularly when they are widowed or infirm, are usually greater than those of young families, and they are often in fairly close contact with at least one child for this reason if no other. Thus the relevance of kinship needs to be looked at in these two different ways. This chapter starts from the viewpoint of the older generation.

The elderly and their kin

The closest form of contact is when people live with kin. So in terms of elderly people the first question is how many of them live with children or other relatives. In 1962 Townsend carried out, as part of a cross-national study (Shanas et al., 1968), a nationally representative sample survey of 2,500 people aged 65 or over in Britain. He found that about a third of the sample lived with children and another one in ten with other relatives, mainly brothers or sisters; few lived with non-relatives. That was over 20 years ago. Direct comparisons cannot be made for later dates because of differences in the various surveys. Despite the limitations, Table II.1 (p.29) compares Townsend's survey with three more recent ones.

The table shows that there has been a dramatic change since the early 1960s. The proportion of elderly people living alone or just with their spouse has risen as the proportion living with children, siblings or other relatives has fallen. Even if one assumes that in 1979-80 all of the 8 per cent living with their spouse and 'others' were with relatives (as the great majority probably were), the total living with kin at that date could have been no more than 20 per cent, compared with the 42 per cent of the 1962 survey. This change undoubtedly reflects an increase in the supply of housing.

If the elderly people less often live with relatives, how near to them do they live? A partial answer - for elderly people living alone - is given by the General Household Survey for 1980 (Office of Population Censuses and Surveys, 1982), in which such people were asked whether they had relatives within five minutes' walk. Nearly a third had.

The best recent evidence about the proximity of children in particular to all elderly people who had them comes from a study by Mark Abrams in 1977 (Abrams, 1978). The survey was in just

11

four urban areas in England and was actually of two samples - aged 65 to 74 and 75 or over - not one. There are other problems when one comes to compare this survey with the Townsend national sample 15 years earlier. Townsend asked whether people had a child in the same household, Abrams in the same dwelling (that is, in the same house or flat but not necessarily sharing fully). The two studies also measured proximity in different ways. But, for what it is worth, Table II.2 (p.30) compares them, showing the proximity of the nearest child to those elderly people who had children but were not living with one. Making the assumption that 'ten minutes' journey or less' correspond roughly to 'same street or neighbourhood', it looks as though the proportion who had children living nearby was probably not very different in 1977 from what it was in 1962.

About a third of the elderly people in Abrams's survey had no living children. He said nothing about whether they lived with or near other kin. The 1980 General Household Survey, like Townsend's 1962 survey, found that some lived with siblings: in 1980 as many as a quarter of single people lived with brothers or sisters - many more than the proportion of married and widowed people doing so. There is, as Townsend put it, a process of compensation at work, people who lack one kind of relative maintaining or redeveloping ties with another by way of substitution. Another study in 1980 - of 134 elderly (65 and over) clients of a London social services department - commented, however, on the limits to the process: 'Although other relatives and friends were important to the client in the absence of children, they were not full substitutes' (Sinclair et al., 1984).

As well as the Townsend and Abrams surveys, figures on frequency of contact from two others are included in Table II.3 (p.31). One is the sample survey by Michael Young and myself in 1970 in the London Metropolitan Region (including Greater London, surrounding country towns and rural areas); about 2,000 people were interviewed, of whom just over 300 were aged 65 or over (Young and Willmott, 1973). The other survey, intended in part as a repeat of Abrams in a rural setting, was done in eight rural areas in North Wales in 1978 and 1979, the sample size being 700 (Wenger, 1984).

The surveys are not strictly comparable and the geographical limitations of all except Townsend's need to be borne in mind. The table suggests that there has probably been a decline in contacts, even when those living with children or other relatives are excluded. But from these and other studies (for example Butcher and Crosbie, 1977) it is clear that there remains a large proportion

12

of elderly people - between two-thirds and three-quarters - who see relatives at least once a week.

Table II.3 confirms that, among those relatives, children are seen more often than brothers and sisters, and two of the surveys also confirm that other kin follow siblings in terms of contact. The London Region survey asked whom the last-seen relative was, and the North Wales study which relative was seen most often. The two sets of findings correspond closely: among all the elderly people (not just those with children or other particular relatives) children were seen most by about half and brothers or sisters by about a quarter, the other quarter being divided between nephews, nieces, cousins and others.

Along with what has been said about the particular importance of siblings to those without children, the kinship research of the 1950s and early 1960s (including Townsend's 1962 survey) reported other patterns of variation among elderly people in their contacts with kin. More recent studies confirm most of those findings.

The general picture is, as it was, that elderly people tend to live with or near relatives more often, and see them more frequently, the greater their need for support and care. The combined General Household Surveys for 1979 and 1980 showed that the proportion of people living with children or children-in-law (but not their own spouse) was one in 20 at ages 65 to 74 but over a quarter at 85 or more. In the London Region survey (1970), the proportion of people aged 65 or over living with kin was three times greater among widows and widowers than among married men or women. In the surveys by both Abrams and Wenger, one urban, one rural, those aged 75 and over saw children more often than those aged 65 to 74, and women saw them more often than men did.

A general bias towards women was also noted in the earlier studies as a strong feature of the kinship relationships of the elderly (and the young). Townsend (1968) said, for instance, that 'Three times as many widowed persons lived with married daughters as with married sons' and that 'Even when living at comparable distances daughters tended to have been seen more recently than sons'. The more recent studies do not show whether elderly people now live with daughters rather than sons. Hunt (1978) found that, among the categories of 'relatives who visited most often', daughters and daughters-in-law outnumbered sons and sons-in-law, and sisters and sisters-in-law outnumbered brothers and brothers-in-law. But the differences were not dramatic and, taken together with the fact that fewer elderly people than in the

1960s now live with daughters (or sons), it may be that the variation is less marked than it used to be. But, as reported next, women continue to provide much more of the informal care given to elderly people than do men.

Kinship care for the elderly

Hunt's survey showed the sources of help to the elderly with the main tasks on which it might be needed. The results in respect of four tasks are given in Table II.4 (p.32). The table shows that most people's toenails were cut by chiropodists, and home helps sometimes did shopping for housebound people. But most help was given by people from the same household (a spouse or a relative) or by relatives living elsewhere. As long as a spouse is alive, and is able to or willing, he or she usually performs such tasks. This apart, relatives are the source of most kinds of help and care, providing more as it becomes more necessary with increasing age and infirmity. Research by Bayley and his colleagues in Dinnington, Yorkshire showed that the elderly people in most need of care received twice as many visits a week from relatives as did those in least need (Seyd et al., 1984). These conclusions are confirmed by a number of other studies (see Office of Population Censuses and Surveys, 1982, Wenger, 1984 and the reviews in Tinker, 1981 and Allen, 1983a).

As just noted, the main carers of elderly people without spouses remain women, particularly daughters and daughters-in-law. Two recent studies, among many, illustrate the point. In a study of 102 elderly people who went for short-stay residential care to provide some relief to the hard-pressed carers, Allen (1983b) looked at who those carers were. Six were husbands or wives. Of the remaining 96, over four-fifths were relatives and over four-fifths of them were women, more than two-thirds being daughters or daughters-in-law. The second study - of the carers of 157 dependent elderly people who had been referred to specialist services (Charlesworth et al., 1984) - found that, excluding husbands and wives, three-quarters of the carers were relatives and three-quarters of these were women. In both studies, reflecting the decline in sharing homes, by no means all the carers were living with the elderly people being cared for: again excluding those living with their spouses, the proportion was half in the first study and a third in the second. In both samples, the relatives living in the same household were mainly women, and again mainly daughters or daughters-in-law.

In considering the care given to some elderly people, it should be borne in mind that most people aged 65 or over are not infirm and that most provide care for others. Wenger (1984) said on the basis of her survey in North Wales that 'there are more elderly providing help of one kind or another than are receiving help', the range given covering the 'full gamut from taking full responsibility for a dependent adult to the triviality of keeping a key for a neighbour's house'. Butcher and Crosbie in their study in Cleator Moor, Yorkshire (1977) noted 'the large proportion of "active" jobs that pensioners do for their children - shopping, small jobs around the house, odd bits of gardening'. But, whichever the direction, most care is within the context of family and kin.

Young people and their kin

The perspective now changes to the younger generation themselves. The main sources of information are a number of 'community studies' done in the 1950s and 1960s and some more recent surveys of particular kinds of people such as married women with young children.

The first question, again, is how many people live with relatives. The proportion of young people living with kin has of course fallen along with that of older. The effects on the young of the changes in the supply of housing have been reported in various studies. A comparison of Banbury at two dates, separated by 17 years, concluded:

Many couples (in 1950) were lucky if they could leave the parental roof when their first child was born ... In 1950, 12 per cent of married men were not household heads, most of them being young married men. In 1967 less than 3 per cent of married men were living in the households of others, and they were evenly distributed among all the age groups (Stacey et al., 1975).

Figures from the Family Formation Survey, covering a longer span and up to a more recent date, confirm the trend. The proportions of married women aged 20 to 49 who, two years after their marriage, were living with others (mainly parents or parents-in-law) fell from 33 per cent among those married in 1955 or earlier to 7 per cent among those married between 1971 and 1975 (Holmans, 1981). Obviously much smaller proportions lived with parents at later stages in their marriage: a survey in five areas in 1970 (Hunt, 1973) found that, depending on the area, from 2 per cent to 4 per cent of married women with children lived with their own parents, and 1 per cent to 2 per cent with their parents-in-law.

Although few younger married people now live with kin a substantial minority, at least, have them living near. Moss and his colleagues (1978) in a survey in 1974 of 340 mothers with children under five in two inner London districts found that about a third had parents 'within walking distance'. Another study by Moss (1983) in 1979, of 85 couples living in a London suburb who had recently had their first baby, showed that two-thirds had parents in the same or an adjacent borough. In a survey of 200 women expecting babies in 1977 in a Northern town, a fifth had parents living within a mile, and over half within five miles (Graham, 1979).

In general, relatives other than parents or children less often lived nearby. Studies of new communities have, however, shown that there siblings - and sometimes more distant relatives of the same generation - are more often present than parents are. Younger people, being more willing than older to move, act as 'pathfinders' to others of the same age.

Physical propinquity is in itself less important than whether relatives see each other. Table II.5 (p.33) gives comparable data from various places on married women's contacts with their mothers. The table shows that the proportion of women seeing their mothers once a week or more varied between about half and three-quarters according to area. The proportions of mothers seen daily are low compared with the 55 per cent seen in the previous 24 hours in Bethnal Green in 1955 (Young and Willmott, 1957) and the 35 per cent in suburban Woodford in 1959 (Willmott and Young, 1960). This suggests that mothers and daughters meet less frequently now than in earlier decades.

There is, however, ample evidence from recent research that parent-child ties in general continue to predominate over others. Moss, for instance, in his London surburb study of couples having babies, said 'Parents were the most likely relatives to be regularly and frequently contacted' (Moss, 1983). Studies that have asked about wider circles show that, as with older people, siblings come next in importance in terms of contact. Firth and his colleagues (1969) found in their study in North London that, in contrast to the links with aunts, uncles, cousins and more distant relatives, virtually all their sample maintained contact in some form with their brothers and sisters.

Allan (1979) has summarised what is known about variations in contact with siblings. People with a number of brothers and sisters quite often have a particularly 'close' relationship with one, often the brother or sister 'closest' in age as well. Wider gaps in age, conversely, tend to reduce contact, as do differences in the stage reached in the life cycle: a women who has had children is, for instance, more likely to keep in touch with her sisters who have done the same than with those who have not. After parents die, contact though maintained is usually reduced, partly because as long as parents are alive siblings often meet at the parental home. As has been noted in discussing the elderly, however, in later life people who are without children often compensate for their absence by closer contacts with their own siblings.

The proportions in contact with any relative, not just parents or siblings, are naturally higher. Between about two-thirds and three quarters see at least one relative at least once a week - similar to the proportions among elderly people. This was true of a sample of London dockworkers in 1969-70 (Hill, 1976), married people with dependent children in the London Region in 1970, mothers of children under five in parts of inner London in 1974 (Moss, 1983), and married people under 50 in Bristol in 1979 (Mitton et al., 1983).

As with elderly people, earlier studies in the 1950s and 1960s reported a female bias in kinship patterns, and above all an emphasis on the mother-daughter bond. Most researchers found that couples tended to live rather nearer to the wife's parent; on the basis of a national survey, Gorer (1955) noted the 'marked tendency towards matrilocality in the English working class'. Women saw their parents, particularly their mothers, more often than men did. They saw their sisters more often than their brothers. In Swansea, where information was gathered about contacts with more distant kin, both men and women saw aunts and uncles on their mother's side more often than those on their father's side (Rosser and Harris, 1965).

Up-to-date evidence about this is once more lacking. As with elderly people, the relative last seen by married people aged under 50 in the 1970 London Region survey was more often a women than a man. The same survey found, however, that in general people saw their fathers as often as their mothers and married men saw both their parents as often as married women saw theirs. Most married couples were in fact together when they met relatives: people's spouses were present at three-quarters of the most recent meetings. Like the evidence on the elderly, this perhaps suggests that, though kinship may remain somewhat more of a female concern than a male, and though women relatives do more for young families as well as for the elderly, in terms of regular contacts the female emphasis may have become less strong than in earlier decades.

Kinship help for the young
Help and support are of course given to the younger generation by the older as well as in the reverse direction. Bell (1968 and 1971) has shown that young middle-class families receive substantial financial support from parents, and that this is related to the family life cycle - parents helping children, for instance, at a stage when they are themselves relatively affluent and children the relatively stretched. In the Banbury study, too, over a third of respondents had received financial help from kin with their housing, the proportion helped being larger among people of higher occupational status.

Most of the earlier studies contain some evidence about practical aid. In Bethnal Green, where kin were so much in evidence, mothers in particular helped their daughters in confinement, with the care of children, in illness and with routine tasks such as baby-sitting. In Acton at about the same time, 'The grandmothers, especially the maternal grandmothers, ... were the childminders for their married daughters who went out to work; they were called in to help in confinement and illness' (Shaw, 1954). The Banbury researchers reported that in 1967 'For locally-born and locally brought-up residents kin members did the baby-sitting'. They added that, as in the earlier Banbury study in 1950, 'In major family crises such as the birth of a baby ... it is the kin, especially the mother's mother, who come'.

More recent research shows that most help with babies and young children is still provided by kin. In a study of 2,400 mothers who had recently had a baby, Daniel (1980) found that in the first month after the birth half had had 'someone to help' (other than their husband or a district nurse or midwife) and that the helpers were overwhelmingly relatives, mainly mothers (69 per cent) or mothers-in-law (20 per cent).

In Moss's study of 85 couples in a London suburb over the period from mid-pregnancy onwards, just over half had relatives staying with them immediately after the birth and another quarter had regular visits at that time. The relatives who stayed or visited were predominantly the babies' grandparents, especially their grandmothers (Moss, 1983).

The Moss study also showed that at six months after the birth two-fifths of mothers were receiving regular help from relatives with child care, mothers helping more often than mothers-in-law. In the Daniel study, among mothers who went back to work and whose babies were cared for by someone other than the mother or father, it was again mainly a relative, usually a grandmother. The 1979 General Household Survey showed that, of the children under

18

five who were regularly looked after by someone other than their parents, about two-thirds were in the care of relatives (Office of Population Censuses and Surveys, 1981). A smaller study of 40 couples in Newcastle and rural Northumberland found that, not only in connection with wives working but in any family crisis, 'the person most likely to take over the housekeeping and child-rearing was the wife's or husband's mother ... Sisters or sisters-in-law were called upon in some cases' (Johnson and MacDonald, 1983).

Moss, echoing Bethnal Green and Acton in the 1950s, found in his study of young families in a London suburb that 'Relatives were far and away the main form of baby-sitting used by parents. They were cited as the most common arrangement by 76 per cent of mothers, with friends far behind (13 per cent) and paid sitters or baby-sitting circles mentioned by only two mothers each'. Relatives were also the main source of advice on child care; they were mentioned by nearly half the mothers (their own mothers once more being the usual person), compared with about a quarter each who said they turned to friends and a similar proportion to health visitors.

There are some exceptions to this general picture, as Chapter VI shows. But it is clear that, at the key stages in life and for most people, relatives contribute essential care as well as helping in more trivial ways. It is equally clear that, even if in terms of sociable contacts the mother-daughter bond is less marked than in the past, most personal care, particularly of a sustained kind, is still predominantly given by women - by daughters and daughters-in-law (and to a lesser extent sisters) to elderly people and by mothers and mothers-in-law (and, again, to some extent sisters) to young families.

The resilience of kinship
Thus kinship remains a major force in the lives of most people. There are negative aspects, of course: the duty visits to in-laws, the conflicts in values and modes of behaviour. Though the role of kinship varies according to circumstances and stage in life - it matters relatively little to young single people, for instance - for most of those who need care, relatives are still the main helpers, and they are also, for most people, valued leisure-time companions.

There have, however, been some changes in kinship in the decades since 1945. The most striking is that the proportion of people sharing a home with relatives has fallen with the increase of housing stock. There has also been more geographical mobility -

more people moving out of their established district, and thus living at a greater distance from their kin. Other changes too have occurred which would seem likely to have worked against kinship. One is a shift in values about the family and about the relationships between the sexes: the changes include a growing emphasis on marital compatibility, companionship and 'symmetry' (Gorer, 1971; Young and Willmott, 1973), the increase in divorce and, more recently, a growing readiness to live together without marriage. A related change is the increase in the proportion of married women working outside the home, from a quarter in 1951 to half in 1981. Though this must have increased the need for child care (much of it provided by kin) the general effect is likely to have been a reduction in their availability to help on a day-to-day basis.

How then has kinship remained as important as it apparently has? The first answer is a reflection of the structure of British - and western - kinship. As has been shown, the system is one in which the main emphasis is on the ties developed between parents and their children, and between fellow-siblings - all members of the same nuclear family. 'Kin groups with such a basis', said Stacey and her colleagues (1975) in explaining the development of kinship among the former newcomers to Banbury, 'can form in a generation: they do not depend upon ancestors beyond parents or at most grandparents, or on a long lineage'. This was also evident in the study of the Dagenham housing estate after one generation (Willmott, 1963). It would therefore be wrong to assume that geographical mobility in post-war decades has caused a permanent and irreversible decline. In some instances public policy, so often criticised for destroying kinship ties, may even have helped to create or recreate them. In 1976 Coates and Silburn did a follow-up study of 141 families previously seen in 1967 in the declining St Ann's district of Nottingham and subsequently rehoused by the local council. They found that contacts with kin were higher than they had been in the old district, and the proportion of people with relatives 'living nearby' had risen from just over half to four-fifths (Coates and Silburn, 1980).

The other main explanation for the resilience of kinship in Britain lies in developments that have made propinquity less important than it used to be. The first of these is the private motor car. As long ago as 1965, Rosser and Harris, studying Swansea, were struck by the relevance of the car to kinship contacts; they commented that the wider family might well be described as 'the motorised family'. Car ownership has increased since then. In 1961 30 per cent of households had a car; by 1984 this had risen to 61 per cent. The proportion of wider families in which somebody has one is obviously even larger. This helps explain why, in both generations, the proportions seeing relatives weekly or more are higher than the proportions with kin living in the locality. The effect of not having a car should, however, also be borne in mind. About two families in five are without one and their relatives will often be similarly car-less. Unless they live within walking distance of each other or are served by excellent public transport, they must find it difficult to maintain frequent contact, and they may even be virtually isolated from kin.

The spread of the telephone has also been influential, among those who have them, in maintaining kinship links. The Woodford study in the late 1950s showed that the telephone was commonly used as a means not only of arranging social visits but also of checking whether there was any need for help. The Banbury study, in 1967, collected systematic information about such contacts: half the married people had met their mother in the previous week, but a further third had been in touch with her by telephone or letter during the same period. The proportion of households with telephones has more than doubled since then - it increased from just over a third to 1969 to nearly four-fifths in 1984. So telephones are used even more fully as links between relatives and, for that matter, friends.

It is thus clear that is is usually not necessary for kin to live in the same 'community' - particularly if this is defined in a highly localised manner - for them to be in frequent and regular contact with each other. Of course, when people live close to their parents and other relatives, kinship is an important element in the local community and personal care by kin is then much easier. But most people's 'community' of kinship is no longer tied to a local territory.

Variations in kinship networks

As has already been shown, this general picture conceals some large differences. Places vary in the proportions of people having relatives near or seeing them often. There are also related differences according to social class and ethnic group.

The variations between places are evident from the more recent surveys, but they also showed up clearly in the earlier local studies and the differences between the areas studied can illustrate some general points. The kinship pattern of the Bethnal Green of the 1950s, for example, differed from that in Woodford at the same date, though the two districts were separated by only a few miles. Bethnal Green was a settled area with a majority of manual workers among its residents. Woodford was a suburb, with a population which was newer, more mobile and more middle-class in the kinds of jobs people did and in other ways. Swansea, also with a sizeable settled population, was rather like Bethnal Green in its kinship patterns. Banbury, with more people moving in and out, was more like Woodford. New communities, like the new towns or the council estate in Essex to which Bethnal Greeners had moved, were extreme cases; everybody was new and few had relatives nearby.

There seem to be three crucial elements at work. One is the age of the district - the period of time over which it has been settled. The second is the extent to which people move in and out. The third is the proportion of residents who are middle class or working class; this is related to the second, because middle-class people are more likely to move district, working-class to stay put. Residential mobility is related to social class because it is affected by people's ability to move if they want to, owner-occupiers finding it easier than tenants, and by whether they need to move for job reasons, movement usually being more necessary to the career advancement of people with professional or managerial occupations. People with higher-status jobs certainly continue to move about more often than others. A recent special analysis of data from the 1973 and 1974 General Household Surveys showed, for instance, that four and half times as many professional and managerial workers as manual workers had moved district during the previous year (Hughes and McGormick, 1985).

The population stability of formerly stable settled working-class districts can be upset, changing their kinship patterns. This has happened in many inner areas as a result of the large-scale clearance and development programmes of the post-war years. Family groups were dispersed and links between kin broken. Evidence from a number of studies - like those in Oldham (Ministry of Housing and Local Government, 1970) and Lambeth (Shankland et al., 1977) - suggests that, if Bethnal Green were studied now, local kinship ties would prove to be weaker than in the 1950s. The findings from Coates and Silburn's study in Nottingham should, however, not be forgotten. Since more people there apparently had relatives near after redevelopment than before, it seems that in some towns a large stock of public housing may facilitate the re-creation of kinship links.

Another change in the social structure of inner areas has been the movement in of immigrants, particularly from the West Indies and the Asian sub-continent. As they have settled, and the second generation has grown up, usually in the same areas, their own kinship networks have developed. A study in the Birmingham inner district of Small Heath found that nearly nine out of ten Asian-born people in the sample had relatives living within ten minutes' walk, compared with about a third in each of the other three main groups in the areas - those born in the United Kingdom, in Eire and in the West Indies (Morton-Williams and Stowell, 1975). It is clear why Asian kin groups have developed in Small Heath and elsewhere, just as West Indian ones have in, for example, Brixton. Migrants commonly go to places where compatriots, particularly kin, have led the way in the same fashion as siblings sometimes join each other in new towns. Members of ethnic minorities tend to stay put thereafter because of the support and protection they receive, in a generally hostile society, from relatives and, more generally, from local ethnic institutions and cultures.

These observations suggest some of the main factors affecting whether kinship is likely in a particular area to be a local affair - that is, whether relatively large proportions of its residents have kin locally, see them frequently and exchange day-to-day support and companionship. As a guide, kinship seems likely to be stronger locally when one or more of the following conditions are present:

- The district has been physically established for a generation or more, that is, it is neither a new community nor a substantially redeveloped one.
- There has been relative stability of population, at least in the sense that some members of the younger generation stay on, close to their parents; this is most likely to occur when one or more of the remaining conditions are met.
- There is access to a range of housing tenures, types and sizes in the district, enabling those who would like to stay to do so.
- There is, in comparison with other places where housing is available, a range of suitable jobs within commuting distance.
- The proportion of manual workers is high, since such people less often move for job reasons.
- The proportion of ethnic minority residents is relatively high, in which case kinship will figure as part of a local ethnic minority community.

Other conditions can also be propitious. When an 'occupational community' is localised - in other words, when a large proportion of people in a town or district work in the same industry

23

or plant, as in a mining village or a dockside area - kinship is relatively strong because the kinship ties of women are reinforced by those of their menfolk sharing the same workplace and job interest (see Lockwood, 1966). It may also be that there is a more general 'traditional' factor: that in some places, relatively cut off from new notions and habits, the established forms of kinship continue to flourish longer than they do elsewhere. As long ago as 1955, Gorer argued that there was a great north-south divide in English kinship, relatives being more scattered in the south, more 'closely-knit' in the north. It is difficult to tell whether this remains true. If it does, the main reason may be that the other conditions are in any event likely to be more common in northern England (or in Scotland or Wales) than in southern England.

The impression from the local studies in the 1950s and early 1960s was that working-class people more often had relatives living near and saw them more frequently. In the London Region survey of 1970 there were some differences by class, but they were not very large. Among manual workers and their wives one in four had relatives living within ten minutes' walk, compared with one in eight among professional and managerial people, and more of the former than the latter had relatives within five miles - three-quarters compared with a third. There was a smaller difference in the proportion of people who had seen at least one relative during the previous week; this was two-thirds among professional and managerial people and just over three-quarters among working class. Thus kinship contacts, at least in terms of weekly meetings, were not much lower for middle-class people despite the distance at which their relatives lived. The explanation was, again, doubtless their cars, supported by their use of the telephone.

Another relevant study is that by Goldthorpe (1980). In his survey, in 1973, 650 men aged 25 to 49 had been selected from an earlier national sample so as to represent different class categories in terms of social mobility and stability. Goldthorpe found some rather larger differences by class than those in the London Region survey. His main interest was in the influence of social mobility on kinship, and on this he concluded: 'There is no clear tendency for kinship relations to be disrupted by mobility'. These two studies therefore suggest that in the early 1970s kinship continued to play a larger part in working-class than middle-class life, but that the contrast was not dramatic and that, in any event, fairly frequent contact was maintained with relatives even among people who had moved up or down the occupational scale.

On the relationship between class and help for kin, the picture is unclear. Some of the results from Goldthorpe's survey in

1973 suggested that relatives provided rather more help for working-class people than middle-class. On the other hand Daniel, in his larger 1979 survey of mothers who had recently had babies, found that the proportion of relatives helping after the birth was 66 per cent in the highest occupational group, 46 per cent in the lowest. And Philip Abrams, on the basis of a survey in 1979 of 173 residents in ten areas of England (carried out as part of a study of neighbourhood care), concluded: 'Overall, the most consistently kin-minded group so far as giving and receiving help were concerned was the highest (in occupational status) and the least kin-minded the lowest' (Abrams et al., 1981).

Perhaps the best way to sum up from these three studies is that current differences by social class and the help provided by relatives are probably not large, and that in certain respects it may now be true that if anything middle-class people give and receive rather more. These various findings - on propinquity, contact and help - run counter to the view, based on the earlier local studies, that kinship was much more salient for working-class people than middle-class. What is not clear is how far the earlier research (including that by my colleagues and myself) drew the wrong conclusions and how far the patterns have changed.

As for ethnic minorities, the tendency for local kin grouping to develop among West Indians and Asians in particular has already been noted. But there has been little research on kinship relationships and how they differ according to ethnic origin, the main exceptions being small-scale studies of pensioners (for instance Berry et al., 1981; Barker, 1984).

Among West Indians one-parent families are more common, and one type of nuclear family, reflecting that in the Caribbean, is based not on a stable relationship between husband and wife but on the tie between mother and her children, often with several fathers (Shankland et al., 1977). In the Caribbean, this pattern, repeated over generations, has been associated with a strong mother-daughter tie and a grandmother-centred family group (an extreme version, as it might be put, of that found in the Bethnal Green of the 1950s). Such wider family groups could not develop among the first generation of immigrants to Britain, because the grandmothers were left behind. There is some suggestion, however, that this pattern is now growing up among West Indians in Britain (Driver, 1982). Among other West Indians, those with nuclear family relationships more like the British norm, visiting and mutual aid between kin are likely to be similar to those described for the general population.

Among Indians, Pakistanis and Bangladeshis, there is strong emphasis on retaining the traditional forms of extended family. This is reinforced by economic co-operation - many Asians being small shopkeepers or traders, who benefit from family support and connections. Kinship thus has, for many Asians, an economic role which is now rare in British society. As for residence, houses are typically occupied by more than one related family, but it has been suggested that single family homes are becoming more common, though still often close to kin and with much contact and support (Ballard, 1982).

A typology of kinship
Another, and final, way of looking at kinship is to distinguish the main kinds of pattern in contemporary Britain. On this basis one can suggest, albeit speculatively, the proportions in each type, and sum up the broad direction of change. In reality the distinctions are less clear-cut, the boundaries more blurred, than is suggested by my simple four-fold typology.

Two preliminary points must be borne in mind. The first is a reminder of the predominance of the nuclear family. People's primary loyalties are to that basic social unit, and ties to kin, however close, take second place. The second is that virtually everybody has some knowledge of kin and some contact with them. If parents, adult children and siblings are alive, contact with them is almost universally maintained if only by letter, Christmas card or telephone, and the same people are usually met (along with more distant kin) at 'rites of passage' such as marriages and funerals. (In a national sample of nearly 1,000 people in 1975, conducted by Mark Abrams and John Hall, fewer than 1 per cent said they had no relatives.)

Within this general context, four main types of arrangement can be identified, the distinction between them turning on the extent to which there are more regular contacts, and the extent to which help and support are provided.

The first type might be described as the local extended family. The term 'extended family' is intended to suggest a group, larger than a nuclear family household, of people related to each other through descent, marriage or adoption. Typically it is composed of two or three families, though there may be more. Typically it is made up of the parents and one or more of their children with their children, but because of the kind of substitution described earlier it might be built around other relationships. Typically the children are daughters, but they may additionally or alternatively be sons. Or, to put it the other way, the

26

characteristic link is through women and their mothers but it can be with their mother-in-laws instead or as well. Physical propinquity is the basis, and these relatives see each other every day or nearly every day. The extended family is the most important social unit outside the nuclear cell.

This arrangement is sometimes described as 'traditional'; it probably still applies to something like one in eight of the adult population of Britain. It is, as suggested, more common among working-class families than middle-class, in stable communities than in those marked by residential mobility or redevelopment, and more in the north of England, the Midlands, Scotland and Wales than in southern England.

The second type might be called the dispersed extended family. This operates somewhat like a local extended family except that it is not local and the meetings are consequently less frequent. The essential elements are that there is regular and still fairly frequent contact, say once a week or once a fortnight, and that support is provided not just in times of crisis but as needed from week to week, including relatively trivial mutual aid such as specialist shopping for each other. Such an arrangement depends, of course, on cars (or a good public transport service) and on telephones. Again, the extended family is typically made up of parents and their married children, and where parents are accessible on both sides there might, from the viewpoint of the younger generation, often be two such dispersed extended families to which they belong. This pattern is at least as common in middle-class as working-class circles. The evidence on frequency of contact suggests that it probably operates for about half the population.

The third type can be described as the dispersed kinship network. The ties between parents and children are again particularly emphasised and siblings, grandparents and grandchildren are also in touch with each other. Contact is maintained with these kin by telephone or letter, and by visits to stay, particularly at Christmas. Members of the network do not give regular help but are called upon when needed, providing (in middle-class circles) the financial aid described by Bell and help from grandmothers and others in illness or at childbirth. Such a kin network may be transformed into the local extended family type when, for instance, an elderly parent becomes widowed or infirm, the parent usually being invited to stay with or near a married daughter or son. The proportion of the population belonging to a dispersed kin network of this kind may be a third at any one time.

The final category could be described as the residual kinship network. Contact is usually maintained by letters or Christmas cards, but relatives are rarely seen. As an effective arrangement for providing care, no kinship structure exists. But this probably applies to a very small minority, say one person in twenty in Britain.

Conclusion

The social changes of the last half-century have by no means eclipsed kinship as a power in people's lives. There has been a reduction in the proportion of extended families that are local, and a corresponding increase in the proportions of extended families and kin networks that are dispersed. Because of technology and improvements in standards of living, propinquity is for most people no longer essential to the maintenance of kin ties or the provision of support. The traditional patterns have been adapted, but kinship continues to play a central role and at crucial stages in life remains the predominant source of care.

Table II.1   Household composition of people aged 65 and over

	Great Britain 1962 %	Great Britain 1973 and 1976 %	England 1976 %	Great Britain 1978 and 1979 %	
Living alone or with spouse only	55	70	74	77	Living alone or with spouse only
				8	Living with spouse and others
Living with children (with or without spouse)	32	15	13	8	Living with children or children-in-law (without spouse)
Living with siblings (with or without spouse)	7	⎫ 13 15	⎫ 13	⎫ 3	Living with siblings (without spouse)
Living with other relatives (with or without spouse)	3	⎬	⎬	7 ⎬ 2	Living with other relatives (without spouse)
Living with non-relatives (with or without spouse)	3	⎭	⎭	⎭ 2	Living with non-relatives (without spouse)
Total %	100	100	100	100	
Number	2,500	7,835	2,622	8,945	

Source: 1962, Townsend 1968; 1973/76, General Household Survey, special analyses by Ermisch and Overton 1984; 1976, Hunt 1978; 1978/79, General Household Survey, in Central Statistical Office 1981.

Table II.2   Proximity of nearest child to people aged 65 and over with at least one child alive (excluding those in same household/dwelling)

	Great Britain 1962 %	Four Urban Areas in England 1977 %	
10 minutes or less	41	38	Same street or neighbourhood
11-30 minutes journey	28	14	Within 5 miles
More than 30 minutes journey	31	48	Further away
Total %	100	100	
Number	1,108	985	

Source: 1962, Townsend 1968; 1977, Abrams 1978. The Abrams figures come from a combination of two matched samples - aged 65-74 and 75 and over - in which the patterns of proximity were similar.

Table II.3 Contacts of people aged 65 and over with children, brothers and sister, and other relatives

	Britain 1962	London Region 1970	Four Urban Areas England 1977	Eight Rural Areas North Wales 1978-79
Of all those with children percentage seeing a child within week	86	-	70	58
Of those with children but not living with a child, percentage seeing a child within week	76	72	64	-
Of all, percentage seeing a brother or sister within week	36	-	24	24
Of all, percentage seeing any relative within week	84	75	-	69
Of those not living with a child or other relative, percentage seeing any relative within week	-	71	-	58
Total number in sample (aged 65 and over)	2,591	323	1,646	696

Sources: 1962, Townsend 1968; 1970, Young and Willmott 1973; 1977, Abrams 1978 (combination of two samples, aged 65-74 and 75 and over); 1978-79, Wenger 1984.

Notes: In the 1962 and 1970 surveys the question was about when children or other relatives had last been seen, and the percentages are of those seen during the week before the interview. In the other two surveys people were asked how often they saw children or relatives, and the percentages are of those seeing relatives weekly or more often.

Table II.4   Sources of help for people aged 65 and over, England 1976

	Bathing	Cutting toe-nails	Going out-doors	Shopping (house-bound)
Percentage of those needing help who received it from:				
Person(s) in household	61	16	57	64
Relative(s) outside	19	5	28	21
Friend(s) outside	5	1	11	11
District nurse/health visitor	9	3	-	-
Home help	2	-	2	13
Chiropodist	-	73	-	-
Other person outside	4	1	5	4
No help received/not stated	4	4	17	3
Number needing help	473	747	243	150

Source: Composite table in Rossiter and Wicks, 1982, from Hunt, 1978.   Percentages add to more than 100 per cent because more than one source was mentioned by some people.

Table II.5   Frequency of contact with mothers (married women with mothers alive)

	Dorset (1970)	Dundee (1970)	Glamorgan (1970)	Halifax (1970)	Haringey (1970)	London Region (1970)	Northern town (1976)	London suburb (1979)
Mothers seen daily	17%	18%	24%	18%	13%	-	14%	-
Mothers seen weekly (London Region - within previous week)	53%	71%	75%	66%	45%	48%	59%	56%
Total number	207	210	367	323	274	219	200	85

Source: Dorset, Dundee, Glamorgan, Halifax, Haringey - Hunt 1973; London Region - Young and Willmott 1973; Northern town - Graham 1979; London suburb - Moss et al., 1978

Notes: Dorset, Dundee, Glamorgan, Halifax, Haringey and London Region - married women with dependent children; Northern town - married women expecting babies, contacts with 'one or both parents'; London suburb - mothers with children under five. 'Weekly' includes 'daily'.

III FRIENDSHIP

Friendship, though also important to most people, is much more difficult to pin down than kinship. People almost invariably know whether their mothers and fathers are alive, and likewise their children, their brothers and sisters, and often more distant kin as well. Once a researcher has established the existence of particular relatives, the task of finding out where they live, how often they are seen and what part they play is comparatively straightforward, subject to the standard caveat about the reliability of information gained in interviews. If friends could be identified as readily - in terms of recognised and easily described relationships to the respondent - the same questions could be put.

This cannot be done. First, the terminology is more ambiguous. There is no agreement about what a friend is, or about how the relationship is to be distinguished from others such as work colleague or acquaintance. It follows that, if you ask me to tell you about my friends, I hardly know whom to include. You will need to explain more clearly what you have in mind.

Researchers have tried to narrow the field in a variety of ways. Some studies concentrate on frequent or recent contacts, asking for example about the number of friends met socially each week or during the previous week, the word 'socially' being defined so as to exclude trivial contacts. Others ask about people's 'best friends', 'closest friends' or, as in one American study, 'very close mutual friends'. Others again start with functions rather than people, asking who is - or would be - turned to for particular kinds of help or sociability; the researcher then asks what the relationship is, one category being 'friend', others being 'relative', 'neighbour' and 'acquaintance'. With all such approaches, however, the word itself remains undefined, so there remain obvious dangers of confusion, ending up by comparing like with unlike.

Three particular ambiguities need to be mentioned. One is that people occasionally describe someone as a friend who is also a relative, a point which was noted for instance by Townsend in his study of elderly people in Bethnal Green (1957). Though one needs to be alert to this possibility, it need not present a serious research problem in practice, since relatives can usually be indentified if necessary.

The second difficulty is about neighbours (itself a problem term, as is shown in the next chapter). People quite often make friends from among their neighbours. It is therefore necessary to recognise that one category of friends is 'friends who began as neighbours'; in this and later chapters, I treat them as far as possible as separate, distinct both from neighbours in the ordinary sense and from friends made in other ways.

The third ambiguity is over the distinction between friendship and friendliness noted in many local studies (see Willmott, 1963; Bulmer, 1986). Friendliness, in the sense of an informal, generalised ease with and warmth towards other local residents is not necessarily associated with high levels of personal friendship, particularly that involving visits to each other's homes.

Despite such semantic problems - the need to draw clear boundaries, and the general danger that people may still define friends differently - the main characteristics of friends can be identified. First, they are normally non-relatives. Secondly, friends are usually people with whom one has a continuing relationship based on sociable contact and on mutual help when needed: one spends some of one's leisure time with them and they are providers and recipients of help and advice. Associated with these, there is, thirdly, usually some degree of affection or emotional attachment.

As already indicated, the main difficulty is that of the threshold. For a particular relationship to count as friendship, how often does one have to meet the person concerned, how much time does one have to spend with him or her? How substantial does any help have to be: advice over which refrigerator to buy, a hand with the redecoration of one's home? And, if the researcher is prepared to venture into the subject, how strong does the sense of attachment have to be?

There are, of course, no 'correct' answers to such questions. The boundaries of friendship cannot readily be defined because there are in reality no sharp distinctions: there is rather a spectrum from undisputed friends at one pole and, moving towards the other, people who are seen relatively infrequently, with whom little or no mutual aid is exchanged and with whom emotional bonds are less strong. At the positive end of the scale, people often distinguish 'close friends' from others, 'close' usually being defined in terms of greater frequency of contact, more help and, particularly, a sense of warmth and intimacy that allows discussion of the most private concerns.

A further complication is that particular friends are not necessarily similarly placed in terms of the dimensions mentioned. For example, as people often explain in interviews, some of their friends, though now inaccessible and therefore seldom seen, are regarded as important and emotionally 'close' on the basis of a past relationship in which there was frequent contact and mutual help. Another example of the complexity is that, again on the basis of past friendship, ties of attachment, of duty, may survive when the friend in question is no longer seen as good company or helpful - or is perhaps not even liked.

Making friends

The last examples touch on fundamental questions about the origins and survival of particular friendships. These are matters on which there is little hard evidence.

The initial development of friendship obviously depends above all upon opportunity. Except in rare circumstances, as for instance with 'pen pals', you cannot make friends with people you have never met. So people's choices are made out of the circles of those with whom they come in contact, for example in childhood, at school, through work, through leisure interests, or through contacts made near their homes.

Obviously, too, one may or may not keep in touch when one's own or other people's circumstances alter. A change in job, a move to another town or district, a marriage, a divorce, the arrival of children - such things may affect the ease of contact, and also offer fresh choices. New friends may be made, old ones lost or discarded. A useful way of looking at a person's current friendships is therefore as something rather like a series of geological strata, representing 'layers' from successive phases of his or her life.

None of this explains why particular people become friends in the first place or remain friends later. One explanation, offered by sociologists such as Blau (1964) and Homans (1961), is in terms of what is usually described as 'social exchange theory' or, sometimes, 'transaction theory'.

As already pointed out in advanced societies like Britain people choose their friends, subject to the constraints imposed by their family, occupational and social background, by their knowledge of and access to others, and by the choices made by those other people themselves. The starting point of social exchange theory is that decisions to become friends with others, or to maintain friendships, are based on a more or less conscious balance of advantages and disadvantages. As Jackson (1977) expressed it: 'The value, or reward, of a friendship to an individual depends on the capacity of the other to provide certain "services" such as emotional support, economic assistance, information, allies and connections and resources outside one's immediate network'.

Many people find this both unconvincing and unattractive as an explanation for the choice of friends and the maintenance of friendship. The relationship is usually experienced as something warm and personal, and the suggestion that one makes and keeps friends because of what one can get out of them does, on the face of it, seem shallow and offensive. But when all the qualifications are added, the case may seem more persuasive.

First, it seems that, even though there is an element of exchange - a reciprocity, as it might be put - in most friendships the calculation of costs and benefits is seldom the initial reason for making friends. The starting point is some kind of mutual attraction or empathy, the basis of which cannot easily be explained. One becomes friendly, to put it simply, with people whose company one finds enjoyable.

Secondly, the notion of the benefit, or potential benefit, to oneself has to be interpreted broadly, as the quotation from Jackson makes clear. The gain enjoyed or envisaged can be much more than economic help or assistance in kind, more even than less intangible benefits such as useful connections with others, advice, encouragement or emotional support. The concept of what one 'gets out of the friendship' should surely be extended further to include the pleasures derived, for instance, from wit and intellectual stimulus. Indeed, it could, by further enlargement, even cover the 'pleasure in a friend's company' just mentioned - though the problem is that the meaning of 'exchange' would then perhaps begin to appear so broad as to be trite.

A third point is that, as Blau explained in putting the case for the concept of social exchange, it differs from economic exchange in that the expected return is usually in terms of 'diffuse future obligations, not precisely specified ones, and the nature of the return cannot be bargained about but must be left to the discretion of the one who makes it' (Blau, 1964). He went on to add:

> Typically ... exchange relations evolve in a slow process, starting with minor transactions in which little trust is required because little risk is involved ... By discharging their

obligations for services rendered, if only to produce inducements for the supply of more assistance, individuals demonstrate their trustworthiness, and the gradual expansion of mutual service is accompianed by a parallel growth of mutual trust (Blau, 1964).

Expressed like this, social exchange theory begins to look more robust. One has only to postulate the contrary view to show that, particularly in its qualified form, it contains a good deal of sense. Under normal conditions would somebody continue to try to develop a new friendship, or go on making the effort to sustain an existing one, if the traffic were wholly one-way, if the relationship was in every respect all give and no take?

There are, however, circumstances in which friendships change. As Blau puts it, the development of mutual trust 'creates a social bond'. The argument can be taken a stage further. When such a bond has existed over a lengthy period of time, it could be suggested, the calculative basis of the relationship may be transcended altogether. As suggested earlier, one may, for instance, go on helping an old friend who is in difficulties long after it has become clear that there is not the slightest chance of return. Or one may visit a friend who is critically ill, not because one enjoys doing it or expects any advantage, but simply because, given the relationship, 'one feels one should'. In both instances, the social exchange basis could be said to have given way to one of 'attachment' (Marris, 1982). The relationship of friendship has become more like one of kinship.

Thus I would argue that the notion of social exchange is a partial explanation for people's decisions to make, and maintain contact with, friends. But it has to be modified to take account of the force of initial attraction and eventual attachment. In an enduring relationship, social exchange is reinforced by - and may be replaced by - a bond of attachment.

Research on friendship
There has been little research on friendship, but some material can be found in the local studies drawn upon in the previous chapter, and in other enquiries. In particular, the London Region survey of 1970 included a series of relevant questions, and new analyses of this material have been carried out for the present report.

A number of preliminary points stand out. The first is that friends, unlike relatives, are commonly of about the same age as each other, and are alike in other ways, such as occupational

38

status, ethnic background and income. Allan, reviewing other studies, says 'Friends tend to be of similar age, sex, class and marital status' (1979). The explanation is that, as already noted, friends are chosen from those who share - or have shared - the same milieus and experience.

Secondly, the research shows the social factors that most strongly influence the number of friends and the pattern of relationships. There are three. They can be summarised as one's social position (usually described in terms of social class); whether one is a man or woman; and one's age or stage in life. In examining the last of these, a rather more differentiated set of distinctions is made in this chapter than the dichotomy between the elderly people and young families adopted in the previous one.

Social class has received particular attention in most British studies. The main conclusions of Allan's review were: first that, whereas relatives dominate working-class sociability, friends dominate middle-class; and secondly that, insofar as working-class people have friends at all, the relationship is radically different: they have particular friends in limited contexts, rather than the kind of generalised friends middle-class people have.

The London Region survey suggests that the first of these propositions is an oversimplification. In the London Region in 1970, contacts with kin did not differ greatly according to social class (as the previous chapter noted) though, as will be shown, professional and managerial people did have more friends than others. The second conclusion - that working-class people either have very few friends or friends of a different kind - has apparently been confirmed in other studies. In Allan's own small survey nearly half the working-class respondents had no friends, compared with about one in ten middle-class respondents. Earlier, Mogey (1956) in his research in a working-class district of Oxford reported that two-thirds had no friends. The research by Michael Young and myself in Bethnal Green (1957) also suggested that friends did not figure much, certainly not as much as kin. Klein's review of the early community studies (1965) remarked that 'Friendship is a category of social behaviour which does not fit easily into traditional working-class life'.

My own view is that the role of friends was probably understated in those earlier studies, and that some general changes in life-styles have in any event reduced such class differences as there were. On the question of interpretation, consider again our Bethnal Green research. Though we rightly said that most people did not invite non-relatives into their homes, we had found - as we reported - that over a third did so. The question we put may, in any case, often have been interpreted by our respondents in over-narrow terms. More than once, on calling back at a house at which it had been reported in an earlier interview that non-relatives were never allowed to enter we met a neighbour having a cup of tea and a chat. (This example illustrates the problem of using survey research alone on such an elusive subject. Sociologists seldom have the chance to observe behaviour in such matters in the way we did over this.) If in the interview we mentioned the apparent discrepancy, the common explanation given was that she was, as it were, not really visiting but had just 'popped in to borrow some sugar' or the like. In addition, we - and other researchers like us - may have shown a cultural bias, laying too much emphasis on sociability inside people's home and not enough on friendships that operated in the pub, club or street. In Bethnal Green, we did not adequately take points like these into account, mainly because we were concentrating on kinship. Had we - and other researchers like us - done so, I believe that friendship might have emerged as more important in working-class life than it did. Furthermore, the patterns of Bethnal Green - where kinship was so dominant - were certainly not universal and, as argued in the previous chapter, are less common now.

It remains true that all surveys show some people to have virtually no friends. Wenger, in a study of elderly people in rural communities in North Wales (1984), found that 15 per cent had 'no real friend' nearby. In the London Region sample, covering adults of all age, 86 per cent reported meeting at least one friend during the previous month (77 per cent during the previous week), but that leaves 14 per cent - one in seven - who had met none during the month (and 23 per cent, or nearly a quarter, who had not met a friend during the week). The same survey showed variations by social class: the proportion having met friends during the previous week was 83 per cent among professional and managerial people, 75 per cent among both clerical and skilled manual and 71 per cent among semi-skilled and unskilled. The proportions are broadly in line with what we had found in the London suburb of Woodford in 1959: there we had used a single manual (working class) and non-manual (middle class) dichotomy; 78 per cent of middle-class people and 67 per cent of working-class (Willmott and Young, 1960) had met one or more friends during the previous week. The conclusions, therefore, are that there is indeed a small minority of people who see little of friends and that there are some differences according to class, but that across the class spectrum a substantial majority meet one or more relatively often.

The limited evidence on ethnic minorities suggests a similar conclusion. One study of 148 elderly West Indians in Nottingham found that 64 per cent had seen at least one friend every day and a total of 83 per cent every week (Berry et al., 1981). Another enquiry, this time of 400 pensioners in inner Birmingham, showed the following proportions having daily contacts with friends: 'Asians', 58 per cent; 'Afro-Caribbeans', 52 per cent; 'Europeans', 48 per cent (Bhalla and Blakemore, 1981).

Sources of friends
Given that most people have friends, the next question is where they come from. In the light of what has already been said, one would expect people to draw their friends from a variety of elements in their past and present lives - school, work, neighbourhood and so on.

Little detailed research has been done on this. Hill's study of 139 London dockers and 93 foremen (1976) showed that the proportion of dock-workers' friends who themselves worked in the docks varied with locality: it was three-fifths in dockside areas and a quarter in other kinds of district. Among foremen the proportions were lower: a quarter and one-eighth respectively. These findings relate to all friends. Hill also found that work was the source for 16 per cent of the 'close friends' of dockworkers as against 4 per cent of those of dock foremen; pubs and clubs accounted for 28 per cent of the close friends of dockworkers and 22 per cent of the close friends of foremen, neighbours for 13 per cent and 22 per cent respectively.

These were all men, in limited geographical areas and in a particular industry. The 1970 London Region survey was of a general sample of the population, covering a whole region and a range of occupation and ages, and including women as well as men. The results of a special analysis from this survey are given in Table III.1 (p.48). The relevant question, asked about the last friend who had been 'met socially', was 'How did you first meet him or her'? Thus the information refers only to one person for each respondent. But it can be assumed that the results show the sources of the kinds of friends who are seen with most frequency, and the table therefore probably reflects the sources of such friends generally in the London Region.

As the table shows, work and neighbours accounted for the largest proportions followed by clubs, churches and leisure contacts. School and university, relatives and other friends also figured as key sources. These findings can be compared with a study in 1972 of 434 new residents and 399 established ones in the

41

new town of Runcorn, where people were asked how they had got to know their friends (Berthoud and Jowell, 1973). The most common source there was neighbours, followed by work. Other sources, all more important for established residents than for newcomers, were relatives, mutual friends and 'pub or club'.

Table III.1 (p.48) shows differences between the sources for men and women. In the London Region, men had met more friends than had women through work and through clubs, church and leisure pursuits; women had met more initially as neighbours and through their children. The sources also varied according to people's stages in life. Neighbours became more important as people got older; at the age of 60 or over, a third of the last-seen friends of men and half those of women were neighbours. Conversely, school and college understandably declined in importance with the passage of time: they accounted for a quarter of the friends of single people aged 29 or under, but for only 3 per cent at 60 or over. Clubs, churches and leisure activities were more important to both young and old than to those in between. The married people in middle life, on the other hand, had more often met friends through their children; in particular, as many as one in seven of married women aged up to 59 had done so.

There proved to be relatively little difference in the London Region survey in the sources of friends according to people's social class (as measured by occupational status), the exceptions being that manual workers and their wives more often had a neighbour as their most recently-seen friend. The proportion was a third among semi-skilled and unskilled manual workers, compared with about a fifth among professional and other white-collar people.

This finding is consistent with what other studies report about neighbours and friends. The first (1950) study of Banbury showed that, 'broadly speaking, in working-class streets near neighbours are the most important sources of friendship' (Stacey, 1960). The study of 'affluent workers' in Luton in 1963 noted 'the propensity of our affluent workers and their wives to limit their friendship relations largely to kin and neighbours' (Goldthorpe et al., 1969). A more recent and much larger national survey - the 1982 British Crime Survey - asked what proportion of people's personal friends lived 'within this area (within about 15 minutes' walk of here).' The proportion saying that 'all or most' lived locally ranged from 15 per cent among professional and managerial people to 34 per cent among unskilled people (figures supplied by Home Office Research and Planning Unit).

Local, non-local and work friends
These findings deal respectively with one friend per person (the London Region survey) and the proportion of friends who were local (the British Crime Survey). But if middle-class people had more friends in total, they might on average have had, numerically, as many local ones. Table III.2 (p.49) shows that this was so in the London Region in 1970.

Professional and managerial people had seen about as many local friends as had manual workers and their wives. That middle-class people have relatively large numbers of local friends should come as no surprise, given the findings from the Woodford study. Describing the middle class there, we said that 'The common pattern ... is to belong to a small, intimate network of "friends", mostly coming from the surrounding twenty or thirty houses'. (Willmott and Young, 1960). This local circle was, we argued, an important source of companionship and practical help, especially for women.

Nevertheless, Table III.2 shows that it accounts for a relatively small part of the total friendship network of middle-class people. It is perhaps surprising that skilled men had more non-local then local friends and the semi-skilled and unskilled about as many. But the most striking finding is that higher-status people, particularly men, had more non-local contacts and in consequence had seen more friends altogether. Another analysis of the London Region survey showed that the numbers of non-local friends were specially high among university and college-educated people. Men among them had seen an average of 9.05 in the week, and women an average of 4.88. This is consistent with a finding from a study of friends in northern California, where the more educated had larger and more dispersed social networks (Fischer, 1982).

The geographically-dispersed friendships of higher-status people are certainly helped by them more often having cars. Further analysis of the London Region data by car-ownership showed that, with men and women taken together, the average number of non-local friends met during the previous week was about two where the household had no car, about four where it had one car and about six where it had two cars.

As well as the difference between men and women shown in Table III.2 - with men in all occupational categories having seen more non-local friends on average than women, and therefore more friends than them in total - there were some differences according to people's stage in life. Young single people saw more non-local friends, and more friends altogether. Single men aged 29 or under, for instance, had seen about eight non-local friends and 12 friends in total during the previous week, whereas men aged 50 and over had seen an average of about three non-local friends and six friends in total. The British Crime Survey (1982) likewise found younger people in the general population having higher contacts with friends.

In the London Region survey the numbers seen during the previous week were also examined in terms of one other category of friends - those 'from your work'. These have been included in the figures already reported; virtually all of them lived more than ten minutes' away and these were counted among the non-local friends. The numbers of such 'work-colleagues as friends' who were seen outside work are shown separately in Table III.3 (p.50). The table shows that the professional and managerial men had seen most work friends, and that among the men the clerical workers had seen fewest. A parallel analysis of this in terms of education showed that university educated men had again seen a particularly large number of work friends - 6.30 - during the week.

Table III.3 shows women, even those who worked, again having fewer contacts than men, this time with work colleagues. This is in line with the evidence in The Symmetrical Family, showing that women were in a range of ways less involved in their employment and its milieu than were men (Young and Willmott, 1973).

Segregation and mixing
Two further questions about contacts with friends concern the extent of mixing, first between men and women, and secondly between people from different social classes.

The patterns of men's and women's friendship suggest that their friends are mainly of the same sex as themselves. In all occupational groups in the London Region survey the most recently-seen friends were predominantly reported as men by men, and women by women.

The general impression this might give of homogeneity and segregation is, however, misleading. Married friends were seen as couples in over half of all recent meetings, even though the husbands presumably thought of other husbands as their primary friends and wives likewise with other wives. There was a social class difference here, the proportion of meetings with couples falling from 62 per cent among professional and managerial people to 48 per cent among semi-skilled and unskilled manual. Other studies, too, report segregation among working-class people between male friendships and female ones. This was noted in a mining village (Dennis et al., 1956), in a Welsh rural area

(Frankenberg, 1957) and among 'affluent workers' in Luton (Goldthorpe et al., 1969). The authors of the Luton study (which was done somewhat more recently than the others) did, however, point out that the segregation was less marked than in earlier research, being in what they described as an attenuated form. This change tallies with the growing partnership between husbands and wives noted by Gorer over a twenty-year period (Gorer, 1955 and 1971). It suggests that over time segregation in the friendships of men and women is declining.

The same may be true of segregation between the classes. The general line in the past has been that few, if any, friendships cross class lines. When studying Woodford at the end of the 1950s Michael Young and I concluded: 'If middle-class people have friends they are usually middle-class people too; if working-class people have friends they are usually working-class too.' Others have said the same. But, as with the earlier point about working-class friendships, this was probably an exaggeration and may anyway have been overtaken by events. There is some evidence of mixing between the classes, particularly if they are neighbours. In his study of dockworkers, for instance, Hill found that half of those living in mixed areas had one or more non-manual friends, compared with a fifth living near to the docks (Hill, 1976). Goldthorpe and his colleagues found that the contacts of Luton 'affluent workers' with 'white-collar' people varied with district (Goldthorpe et al., 1969). Among the non-kin 'spare time companions' of those living in 'middle-class' or 'lower middle-class' areas, a fifth were white-collar people, compared with one in ten on council estates; and about a quarter of the former as against a tenth of the latter were entertained at home. Goldthorpe also found that people who had white-collar links through parents or parents-in-law, or through the wife's job, more often had sociable contacts with white-collar people.

But the general points made earlier stand. Friends more often come from similar kinds of people to oneself, and differences remain by class, by stage in life and whether one is male or female.

Why class differences?
The differences between men and women, and those between people at different phases in the life-cycle, are easy enough to understand. They turn on opportunity. Women still tend to spend more time in and around the home than men do, and so see fewer work friends and non-local friends. Likewise those with children are often restricted to the locality, as are elderly people.

The differences between the classes are more difficult to explain. One view of class differences in friendships has been mentioned earlier. Allan argues that working-class people do not make 'general' friends, in the same way as middle-class; on this view, they have more limited friendships tied to particular contexts - people are neighbours or work friends, fishing friends or pub friends (Allan, 1979). Much the same point had been made earlier by Goldthorpe (1969). And it meshes with Hill's finding that most of the social contacts of his dockworkers were casual ones, over 90 per cent being in pubs.

How can such class differences be explained? One suggestion, put forward for example in the Woodford study and mentioned in an earlier chapter, is in terms of 'social skills'. Middle-class people, it is argued, have had to move more often for career reasons. This has meant leaving behind relatives and the familiar local community. Needing social networks, they have had to devise methods of getting to know people relatively quickly. They also join clubs and associations more often than working-class people (see for example Young and Willmott, 1973). They make friends at work and through work and professional contacts. From among the people they meet, they choose to develop relationships extending beyond the initial narrow interest.

Working-class people, so the argument continues, have not usually developed such skills because they have not needed to. So, when they do need to, they are ill-equipped, lacking the experience and hence the necessary confidence. On this interpretation, working-class people who have moved district are particularly likely to be relatively isolated. This is indeed what, back in the 1950s, we argued had happened among the people who had moved from Bethnal Green to the new suburb of Greenleigh; Goldthorpe and his colleagues said the same about the migrants among their Luton manual workers and their wives in the 1960s .

As to the applicability of such arguments now, it is difficult to speak with any confidence. More working-class people have moved district in the last two decades, and more of them have moved to mixed-class districts, where they may have emulated their middle-class neighbours. The occupational structure has also changed, with the proportion of white-collar - and white-overall - jobs increasing, and that of low-skill manual jobs decreasing. It seems reasonable to suppose that the differences between the classes are narrowing. As with kinship, this is likely to be happening faster in some regions and in some kinds of district than others, so that in some places the friends of working-class people remain relatively few, relatively segregated as between men and women, and more often seen in a limited context rather than being 'general' friends.

Conclusion

Friends are clearly important to almost everybody. But they present something of a paradox when compared with kin. In terms of social contacts friends usually play a bigger part. A comparison of data relevant to the last chapter and this one shows that, in the London Region in 1970, men had met an average of 7.59 friends during the previous week but 2.94 relatives, and women 4.57 friends as against 2.61 relatives. In that study the predominance of friends over kin was particularly marked among the young but it applied to a greater or lesser extent to people of all ages and at all stages of life. Other research confirms the general conclusion: friends are more common leisure companions than relatives.

In terms of help the bias is the other way. As the previous chapter showed, at the critical stages, such as in old age or infirmity or when babies are born, relatives outnumber friends as sources of support in the ratio of about ten to one. The same predominance of kin has been noted in studies of those who cared for others in terminal illness (Cartwright et al., 1973) and of those who supported people who had recently been bereaved (Bowling and Cartwright, 1982).

There are exceptions to the general rule. Just as childless people turn instead to siblings, or other kin, so people without relatives compensate to some extent for their absence by seeing more of, and getting help more often from, friends (Hunt, 1978). In particular, as mentioned earlier, young families who live at a distance from relatives often depend on local friends of about the same age in the same way as people used to look to kin in traditional areas for help with baby-sitting, shopping and support in their own or a child's illness (Willmott and Young, 1960).

The balance between different sources of care, and the circumstances in which one kind of source is drawn upon rather than another, are discussed more fully in a later chapter. Meanwhile, the point to be noted is that, despite the important role of friendship socially, most people do not turn to friends when serious continuing demands are likely to be placed on them. If at all possible, they look to relatives instead. For such purposes, friends are seen as second best.

47

Table III.1　　Sources of most recently-met friends (London Region, 1970)

	Men %	Women %	Men and Women %
Work or work interest (including spouse's work)	32	27	29
Neighbour (including former neighbour)	20	31	26
Club, church, leisure	19	11	15
Through Relatives	9	10	9
Through school, university college	10	7	8
Through friend	6	4	5
Through child	2	6	4
Other source	2	4	3
Total %	100	100	100
Number	837	889	1,726

Source:　Special analysis of London Region survey (Young and Willmott, 1973).

Table III.2   Average numbers of local and non-local friends met socially during previous week (London Region, 1970)

	Professional and managerial	Clerical	Skilled manual	Semi-skilled and un-skilled manual	All
Men					
Local friends (living within ten minutes' walk)	2.93	2.36	2.91	3.16	2.89
Non-local friends	7.59	3.03	4.12	3.14	4.70
Total friends	10.52	5.39	7.03	6.30	7.59
Number	245	126	350	186	907
Women					
Local friends (living within ten minutes' walk)	3.06	1.46	2.51	2.05	2.39
Non-local friends	3.31	2.53	1.69	1.44	2.18
Total friends	6.37	3.99	4.20	3.49	4.57
Number	239	149	366	191	945

Source: Special analysis of London Region survey (Young and Willmott, 1973).

Table III.3   Average numbers of work friends met socially during previous week (London Region, 1970)

	Profess-ional and manage-rial	Clerical	Skilled manual	Semi-skilled and un-skilled manual	All
Men	2.92 (215)	0.52 (113)	0.92 (296)	0.97 (159)	1.41 (783)
Women	0.76 (119)	0.65 (103)	0.64 (183)	0.22 (85)	0.59 (490)

The numbers are shown in brackets.
Source: Special analysis of London Region survey (Young and Willmott, 1973).

Virtually everyone has neighbours in some sense, even people who live on remote farms - indeed neighbours are particularly important to them. In urban and rural areas alike, 'nigh-dwellers' (in the Anglo-Saxon phrase Philip Abrams often used) commonly play some role.

On the face of it: 'Neighbours are quite simply people who live near one other', as Philip Abrams said in opening a detailed report in which he showed that the subject was a good deal more complicated (see Bulmer, 1986, a posthumous collection of Abrams's writing on neighbours and neighbouring). As with relatives and friends, problems of overlap and semantic confusion arise.

A particular ambiguity, referred to in the previous chapter, is about friends who are also neighbours. Townsend (1957) reported that the elderly people he interviewed in Bethnal Green described a neighbour who had become a friend as a friend, so that for them a neighbour was a person who lived nearby but was not a friend. As suggested in the discussion of 'local friends' in the previous chapter, it probably serves the interests of clarity if one accepts the distinction made by Townsend's respondents and to regard neighbours who are friends as falling into a particular category of friend. To do this would also be to follow the American sociologist, Suzanne Keller, who in a book about 'the urban neighbourhood' (1968) said firmly 'If you become good friends with your neighbour, the friendship relation usurps the neighbour relation'. If this is accepted, the term 'neighbour' is reserved for those living nearby with whom the relationship is different from - and less than - friendship as that is usually understood. As will be seen later, however, this logical distinction cannot always be maintained in reporting studies of friends and neighbours, any more than it can in ordinary conversation, so that some ambiguity and uncertainty are bound to remain.

Another conceptual difficulty, rather like the one of defining friends, concerns the boundaries: how far from your own home do you stretch your notion of a neighbour? Next door, half a mile away or somewhere in between? In 1982 Market Opinion and Research International (MORI) carried out an opinion survey for the Sunday Times on the subject of neighbours, with a national sample of 1,800 people (Lipsey, 1982 and MORI, 1982). When they were asked how they defined their neighbours in terms of propinquity, 36 per cent opted for next door, 36 per cent the same street or block of flats, 22 per cent within a few nearby streets and the remaining 6 per cent a larger area.

It looks therefore as if people are divided. The trouble with such 'forced-choice' questions is that they often suggest over-simple conclusions. My own view, based on impressions from interviews, is that, although respondents will if pressed choose one of the proffered options, most recognise that, unfortunately for clarity, the term neighbour is called on to do multiple duty. In the narrowest sense, neighbours are just the people next door: as it is often put, the 'immediate neighbours' (a term which itself recognises the semantic problem). Next is the concept of a rather wider circle, those within, say, a dozen houses of one's own. Thirdly, there can be a still wider catchment, covering the same street plus perhaps one or two adjacent streets. Most urbanites probably see themselves as having neighbours of these three different kinds.

Contacts with neighbours

The 1982 MORI survey also asked a range of questions about people's knowledge of and relationship with neighbours, defined for this purpose as 'people living in or near the same road/flats as yourself'. The survey found that almost everybody knew some of their neighbours by name, just 2 per cent knowing none and 3 per cent only one. Nearly half knew eleven or more. People who had recently moved in usually knew fewer than others but, even among those who had lived in the district for less than a year, as many as a quarter knew eleven or more.

Nearly two-thirds of the sample said they spoke to one or more neighbours every day, and over nine out of ten did so at least once a week. Likewise nearly nine out of ten people in the MORI survey said their neighbours were 'friendly'. (The point made in the previous chapter about the distinction between 'friends' and friendliness' applies particularly in connection with neighbours. When people say they find the neighbours 'friendly' they mean to suggest a generally cordial atmosphere, not that they are or would expect to be personal friends with those under discussion.)

Limited though the indices may be, the MORI results certainly do not suggest a high degree of social isolation. Other studies confirm the findings. In a survey of the Bourneville estate near Birmingham, Sarkissian and Heine (1978) found that nearly nine out of ten people knew by name 'all' or 'nearly all' their close neighbours ('the half-dozen families who live closest to you') and a similar proportion talked to one or more of them 'several times a week'. In the study of elderly people in eight rural areas in North Wales cited earlier (Wenger, 1984) 96 per cent said that they got on well with all or most of their neighbours, and 91 per cent talked to neighbours regularly. In the 1980 General Household Survey, four-fifths of a national sample of over 4,000 people aged 65 or over talked to neighbours at least once a week. Among 400 pensioners in inner Birmingham, two-thirds of 'Afro-Caribbeans' had definite contact with neighbours as had half of 'Asians' and of 'Europeans' (Bhalla and Blakemore, 1981) and only one-tenth said they did not know a single neighbour to talk to.

For many people, neighbourly contacts go beyond an exchange of words in the street. The MORI survey asked how often people visited the home of a neighbour and how often any neighbour came in to them 'for a chat'. About two people in every five said that they went in to their neighbours weekly or more often, and rather more - nearly half - reported neighbours coming in the same frequency. (There is no obvious explanation for the variation in proportions with the two questions. It might have turned on differences of wording - a few people, for instance, thinking of 'visiting' as somewhat more formal than 'calling round'. More likely it reflects a general propensity, evident elsewhere in surveys, to suggest that one gives rather more than one receives, in this case of hospitality.)

There were, in any event, similar patterns of answers with both questions. The proportion visiting neighbours was, for instance, higher among women (about half) than among men (about a third); lower for people aged 24 or under (about a third) and higher for people with young children (about half). The reasons for these variations are clear enough. Women spend more time in the home and the locality than men do. Young people are less home-bound than older people, and those with children are particularly likely to be tied to the neighbourhood.

There were also some differences between the social classes. These are shown in Table IV.1 (p.64) in terms of both visiting and being visited. The table suggests that, although there is a larger working-class minority than middle-class who neither visit neighbours nor have them in their homes, when they do visit or are visited by them, they do so at least as often as middle-class people. This is relevant to the general point in the last chapter about the extent to which working-class people went into the homes of non-relatives. I argued there that the earlier research probably exaggerated the working-class resistance to friends entering the home, and also that, though class differences remained, such resistance had probably weakened over time. The same seems to be true of neighbours.

In the MORI survey, neighbours came in for a drink or a meal less often than they 'called round': less than half the sample had ever provided neighbours with drinks and a quarter with a meal. Here the class differences were more striking than those just reported: nearly twice as many people in the 'top' category as the 'bottom' had neighbours in for drinks, and three times as many for meals.

Neighbours as friends
In interpreting such findings, there is still the terminological problem. It seems likely that, in terms of the distinction introduced earlier, many of the 'neighbours' reported by MORI as coming in for a meal or being drinking companions in a pub would be thought of by people themselves not as neighbours in the narrow sense but rather as friends who had been recruited from among neighbours - as people who had been neighbours but were now something more. The networks of local friends developed in places like Woodford were mentioned in the preceding chapter; one of the women there certainly thought of some of those in the same road as her friends rather than neighbours:

> I've got a lot of friends, most of them in Corncroft Crescent. There's Mary at number 4, Eileen at 16, another friend at 24, another at 29 and another at 21 (Willmott and Young, 1960).

Woodford is a largely middle-class suburb but a similar pattern was observed in the working-class housing estate at Dagenham studied at about the same date (Willmott, 1963), and in other studies of council estates (for example Mitchell et al., 1954; Hole, 1959) and of the new town of Stevenage (Willmott, 1962). Two Dagenham wives illustrate the point:

> We've got some good friends, particularly Mrs Gordon over the road and Mrs Wheeler who lives just down the street. If I'm ever fed up I go in to Mrs Gordon for a friendly cup of tea and a chat and then we go to Mrs Wheeler, the three of us are just like that.

I've got two good friends. Mrs Barker, who lives opposite, has got a spin drier and I've got a sewing machine. I put my washing in her spin drier and she uses my sewing machine when she wants to. Then the lady next door on one side is another friend of mine. We always help each other out.

One does not, and cannot, know how many of the MORI respondents, if asked explicitly about the matter, would have followed the women of Woodford and Dagenham in describing as friends rather than neighbours some of those 'living in or near the same road'. The difficulty of interpretation can only be noted. The importance of the various findings stands: in present-day Britain the overwhelming majority of people know their neighbours and are on reasonably good terms with them, and most have sociable contacts, often substantial ones, with some of their neighbours.

A delicate balance

There is, however, the negative side. Neighbours do not always get on with each other: there is 'bad' as well as 'good' neighbouring. The MORI survey asked people whether they had 'had any kind of problems in your dealings with any of your neighbours over the last two years'. One person in five had had such problems. The main subjects of discord were noise (mentioned by over a third), pets (a fifth) and children's behaviour (about a fifth). People with children more often reported problems (between a quarter and a third did so); people aged 65 or over less often did so (one in ten). There were no class differences.

Such complaints illustrate one of the characteristic features of the neighbour relationship. Since neighbours are the people who happen to live near you, you cannot change them - except by moving - and for the most part you therefore have to come to terms with them, and they with you. This applies particularly, of course, to the immediate neighbours; those living further away matter less in this respect. The problem was illustrated in the study of the Dagenham council estate where there were, for instance, sometimes quarrels over the cleaning of shared porches and conflicts between older people and their neighbours over children's play.

Because of the ever-present risk of disputes and tensions, people lay emphasis on the need for privacy and reserve, alongside the general disposition towards friendliness reported earlier. The point emerges from many studies of neighbours. For example:

Great value was placed on helpfulness, such as practical assistance in times of illness or keeping an eye on children when the mother was out. At the same time there was an almost equal emphasis on withdrawal. The ideal neighbour was neither too interfering nor too intimate, and did not repeat confidences (Hole, 1959).

What people said they wanted from their neighbours varied from person to person, but mostly involved a balance between their being friendly and helpful and their not being intrusive (Llewelyn-Davies et al., 1977).

On the basis of his review of the research on neighbouring, Philip Abrams concluded:

There is one feature of neighbouring which seems to be enormously valued as a component of positive neighbouring, respect for privacy. So regularly and emphatically does this emerge from the literature that it must be placed alongside friendliness and helpfulness as one of the essential components of positive neighbouring ... Two of these elements seem to be essentially sociable and other-regarding; the third is plainly disengaging and self-regarding. Good neighbouring could be said to be a matter of finding a point of equilibrium in a highly unstable field of contrary forces (Bulmer, 1986).

The dilemma is clear enough. People want to get on with their neighbours. If they can do so life is pleasanter and less stressful than it would otherwise be. Neighbours will also be able to do useful small services for each other as needed. People want, however, to preserve the privacy of family life, and to admit others to their homes only as a matter of choice. Most neighbours recognise all this, but some may not. If the neighbours turn out to be inquisitive, over-enthusiastic about entering the homes of others, inclined to gossip, liable to stir up trouble, the relationship will turn sour. Hence the need to maintain the proper balance - the 'equilibrium', to use Abrams's word - reasonable warmth and the proper degree of reserve.

Help between neighbours
The help given by neighbours to each other can vary widely. In rural areas, for instance, neighbourly help seems to be more common than in towns; in the study of elderly people in rural Wales

only 2 per cent felt that there was no neighbour from whom they could ask favours (Wenger, 1984), compared with 10 per cent in a national sample of elderly people (Hunt, 1978). Other studies show a high degree of neighbourly help in villages and also among farmers, who freely borrow and lend machinery and equipment (Williams, 1956 and Frankenberg, 1966). Another extreme example of neighbourly help is in major natural disasters such as floods; an American study noted that in such disasters neighbours rescue as many as three-quarters of those rescued (Barton, 1969).

In the ordinary round of life the help takes more mundane forms. The MORI sample survey indicates the kinds of things often done. People were shown a list of possible forms of help and then asked whether 'you or members of your household have helped any of your neighbours over the last year or so' and whether help had been given in the reverse direction (Table IV.2, p.65).

The tendency to suggest that one does more for neighbours than they do for oneself can again be noted. The main point from the table is that the great majority had both given help and received it. Help was most common over looking after keys, looking after pets and plants, borrowing food and shopping, but the proportions are relatively large also with help with house maintenance or repairs, help in illness and looking after children (around half of those who had children helped and were helped with them). Death in the family is rare; when this is taken into account, even the proportion of helping over that is fairly high.

There were some differences between types of people, in addition to the point just noted about families with children. A particular kind of family - that of lone parents and children - gave and received more help than other people in the sample in terms of loans of food, shopping, help in illness and help with children. Younger people and elderly people exchanged less help generally, though the differences were not dramatic. (The position of elderly people is discussed more fully later.) Newcomers, as one would expect, gave and received less help than others.

Despite the fact that higher-status people more often move district for job reasons, the findings on social class went the other way. The 'highest' class people both gave and received most help and the 'lowest' class least, except over shopping and illness. Owners likewise helped each other more than tenants, and those living in houses more than those in flats. Thus contrary to the stereotype, middle-class suburbanites were more 'neighbourly', in this sense, than working-class inner-city dwellers. Some of the same points emerge from other research, including an intensive small-scale study by Colin and Mog Ball (1982) and the work by

Philip Abrams in 1979 and 1980 in ten areas having neighbourhood care schemes (Abrams et al., 1981). In interviews with samples of residents in the ten areas, more peole said they gave help to neighbours (79 per cent) than received it (66 per cent). People in mid-life - in their forties - gave and received most help. Higher-status people did more than lower.

The Abrams study, unlike the MORI survey, was however not purely statistical, and it provided examples of help beyond the limited MORI list. As Philip Abrams explained, the needs met were largely ones:

> ... that arose quickly, required quick alleviation and were not dependent upon specific technical or occupational skills. A short list from many similar replies exemplified the sort of tasks that fall into this category: 'We just borrow from each other when we're short'; 'we do gardens, post letters, collect papers - that sort of thing'; 'baby-sitting, lending tools, help dig out drains, transport to the supermarket'; 'we knit for the neighbours and lend them tools, keep an eye on old people and the wife visits them for company'; 'we have a neigbour's child from school when she has to work in the afternoons'; 'we take in the post and keep a key when they're not there - sometimes take the milk in'; 'I always have a key for next door and opposite when they go away on holiday - I go in to see if the houseplants are alright' (Bulmer, 1986).

Abrams went on to argue that in essence neighbourly help depended upon proximity and the ability to respond over trivial matters - 'if it's raining we take in the washing' - or over major or minor crises - 'I helped my neighbour next door when her husband died and the woman next door when she was ill'. But he also reported that sometimes people gave 'long-term and continuous care to their neighbours'. Examples were: 'I look on my neighbour as a daughter ... and she probably thinks of me as a mother'; 'We have helped an elderly couple next door for years - we make sure they're all right. We pay their milk bill and exchange papers and I go shopping for them. My husband also put a bell in their house that rings in our place which they can use if ever they need us'.

Neighbourly care for the elderly
The discussion of care has so far been mainly in terms of people of all ages, though some points about the life cycle have been made. For example, young single people neither give nor receive much

neighbourly support; and families with children, including in particular single-parent families, give and receive more than others. Both these sets of findings are as expected, the first because single people have relatively few needs that could be met through neighbourly care and are relatively free of ties to the immediate locality, the second because people with children are on the contrary more tied to the neighbourhood and are also at a stage when they are likely to need help. The other main category of people who might need help are the elderly, and neighbourly care for them deserves special attention.

Apart from the kinds of neighbourly help already mentioned, the MORI survey asked a further question: 'Are there any old or disabled people in this neighbourhood whom you keep an eye on to see if they need help?' Nearly a third replied affirmatively, the overwhelming majority doing so in terms of non-relatives. Most of the people helped in this way were 'just neighbours', but one in seven had been brought to people's notice by other neighbours, friends or relatives and one in ten by a church, social club or voluntary organisation.

Men 'kept an eye' on elderly people as often as women. Few people aged 24 or under did so (one in every five), and those aged 45 to 65 did so most often (two in every five), but people themselves 65 or over did so as often as those aged 25 to 44 (just under a third). New residents, again, less often did so. There were no differences by social class.

This sort of contribution by neighbours was noted by Sinclair and his colleagues in their study of elderly clients of social services in a London borough. They found what they called 'surveillance', together with general friendly contact, to be the most important role of neighbours in helping elderly people:

> Neighbours were the people likely to be on hand in case of emergency. In about half the cases they were important in terms of keeping a regular eye on the old person and having friendly contact with them (Sinclair et al., 1984).

The same researchers found that, as usual, people's own children were the main carers, but they identified things that neighbours were particularly likely to do:

> In a third of the cases, we rated a neighbour as being the most important source of companionship for the old person ... In a third of cases, neighbours linked the client with the outside world (for example, doing some shopping or collecting

a prescription). They provided some practical help ... Neighbours were almost never the recipients of the clients personal confidences.

People's contacts with neighbours have been discussed in general terms earlier. As the study just quoted shows, such contacts may be of special importance to elderly people who would otherwise be cut off. The MORI survey found that people over 65 had 'neighbours calling round for a chat' rather more often (54 per cent weekly or more) than younger people did (45 per cent), and as many older as younger people - nine-tenths - reported speaking to neighbours weekly or more. The findings from the 1980 General Household Survey put a rather different complexion on the matter (Office of Population Censuses and Surveys, 1982). The overall proportion saying they talked to neighbours at least once a week was four-fifths, not very different from MORI's nine-tenths, and the General Household Survey also found that people living alone talked to their neighbours as often as did those living with others. But in comparing elderly people of different ages over 65, as MORI could not do because of numbers, the GHS reported a decline in contacts as people became older. Thus the great majority of elderly people have some contact with neighbours, but the small minority who lack such contact increases with advancing age and infirmity.

The earlier quotation from Sinclair and his colleagues showed that, although 'surveillance and friendly contact' were particularly common, some of the people in their study also received practical help from neighbours. The MORI results on various forms of help show how elderly people compared with others. In several respects they did less for neighbours and received less from them than younger people did, but most of these differences seem to be explicable in terms of elderly people having less need for the help or being less able to offer it. For example, they obviously seldom received help with children and they seldom gave it and, though they received less help with keys and pets, this may have been because they less often went away on holiday. They did, however, receive more help with shopping and more help in time of illness than did younger people: of the people aged 65 or over the MORI sample two-fifths had had shopping done for them and a third had been helped in illness.

So the picture of help from neighbours to elderly people is a mixed one. They provide 'surveillance' for some elderly people and some practical help to others. It is impossible to make any judgement about how far what is done is adequate to meet the 'needs' of elderly people, but it seems likely that some such needs remain unmet.

One of the reasons is a reluctance to seek help, especially when it cannot be reciprocated. Leat (1983), reporting a study of help by neighbours for elderly people in three areas, said: 'The independence of the elderly as a barrier to neighbourly helping was a theme in all three areas'. In line with the general point about privacy made earlier in the chapter, Sinclair el al. commented that 'Clients were reluctant to ask neighbours to do things for them and they were careful not to divulge private matters to their neighbours or exhaust their neighbours' goodwill by asking for favours without giving anything in return'.

Some elderly people apparently feel reluctant even in an emergency. Hunt (1978) asked a specific question about the number of neighbours elderly people would 'feel able to ask' if they 'ever needed help urgently'. Though most said they could ask at least one, and two-fifths said three or more, one in ten (as noted earlier) said they would not feel able to ask anybody; this rose to one in eight among people aged 75 or over.

For elderly people needing help or care, it might be thought that their reserve, and the reduced contact and support that go with it, do not matter too much because of the kind of compensation mentioned in the chapter on kinship - people who see little of neighbours perhaps being mainly those with relatives or friends at hand. It is unfortunately clear that things do not work like that. Abrams and his colleagues (1981) found that the clients (of all ages) of the neighbourhood care schemes studied did not always have kin contacts in place of those with neighbours: 'Isolation appears in many ways to be a self-aggravating condition'. Likewise, in the 1980 General Household Survey 'those who had frequent contact with relatives or friends were more likely to talk to their neighbours than were those who had little contact with relatives or friends' (Office of Population Censuses and Surveys, 1982). The same report showed that compensation sometimes did happen: 'Even among those who did not see relatives or friends at all ... two thirds talked to neighbours at least once a week'. That still left, of course, one third who did not.

Variations in neighbouring

Neighbours are clearly more important in the lives of some people than of others. Elderly people are one example, which is why they have been considered separately, and families with dependent children have been mentioned as another. There is, as Hallman (1984) points out, an ebb and flow through the course of the life cycle, with certain stages when much of life is constrained within the locality - and neighbours are potentially important - and others when the locality, and neighbours, matter less. Childhood, early parenthood and old age are examples of the first type of phase; adolescence, early adulthood and middle age of the second. At any age people who lack adequate private or public transport - as is true of many housewives - are likely to be more tied to locality, as are the physically and mentally handicapped. Neighbours also figure more in women's lives than men's, with more of them being at home with young children or as housewives and more of them being elderly (because of women's greater longevity).

Some other differences have been mentioned. When people are relatively new to a district they have less to do with the neighbours, for obvious reasons. There is also the variation between social classes, which seems again to turn on the skills associated with past residential mobility.

In addition people in all classes differ among themselves in their readiness to mix with neighbours, and above all in the willingness to help them. One can talk of differences in personality, in confidence, in preferences. Finally there is what Philip Abrams described as:

> The sense of family traditions of neighbouring reported by so many informants in so many studies. People appear to re-enact the forms of neighbouring they learned to regard as normal during their own childhood. They refer again and again to what their mothers did or what it was like 'when I was a child' as a norm for their own practice in later life. And this invocation of the past as a guide to the present seemed to be particularly marked among those particularly caught up in positive neighbouring, those most likely to be judged 'good neighbours' (Bulmer, 1986).

Conclusion
Relationships with neighbours are characterised by a mixture of friendliness and reserve, though neighbours sometimes become personal friends, and trust and openness then take over. Neighbours are an important source of certain kinds of help, most of which derive precisely from the fact that they are close at hand. 'Surveillance' is one example. Others are the kinds of tasks mentioned by Abrams - meeting needs that arise quickly and require quick alleviation, including help in emergencies large and small.

This discussion opens up two wider sets of issues. One is about distinctive differences between the kinds of relationship reviewed in this and the two previous chapters: how do kinship, friendship and neighbouring compare, particularly in the kinds of care they can provide? This is one of the subjects of the next chapter. The second question is about the relevance not just of neighbours but more generally of neighbourhood and local community in people's lives in contemporary Britain, a question taken up in the subsequent chapter.

Table IV.1   Visiting neigbours and neighbours 'calling round for a chat' according to social class (Britain, 1962)

	'AB'	'CI'	'C2'	'DE'
		Social	Class	

Percentage visiting the home of
any of the neighbours:

	'AB'	'CI'	'C2'	'DE'
Weekly or more	38	42	42	42
Less than once a week	41	34	28	21
Never	21	24	30	37
Total	100	100	100	100

Percentage 'any of the neighbours calling round for a chat':

	'AB'	'CI'	'C2'	'DE'
Weekly or more	41	45	50	50
Less than once a week	40	32	23	18
Never	19	23	27	32
Total	100	100	100	100
Number	319	419	534	501

Source: Market and Opinion Research International (MORI), 1982.
Note: Neighbours are defined as 'people living in or near the same road/ flats as yourself'.

Table IV.2   Help to and from neighbours in 'last year or so'
(Britain, 1982)

	Help to neighbours	Help from neighbours
Looked after house key for tradesmen to get in/ emergencies	53%	47%
Looked after pets or plants	44%	40%
Helped out with items of food when they/you ran out unexpectedly	41%	30%
Shopping	40%	32%
Provided help or advice in household maintenance/repairs	39%	29%
Helped out during times of illness	36%	28%
Looked after children (among those with children)	32% 50%	24% 51%
Helped out when a family member or close friend died	17%	10%
None of these	14%	20%

Source: Market and Opionion Research International (MORI),
1982 (Sample size: 1801).
Note: Neighbours are defined as 'people living in or near the
same road/flats as yourself'.

V PATTERNS AND DEFICIENCIES

The picture that begins to take shape from the three previous chapters is incomplete. One omission is personal relationships besides those with kin, friends and neighbours.

One such example is work colleagues, contacts with whom are certainly face to face and often substantial. Relationships between colleagues sometimes develop in affection and trust, involving the exchange of confidences and the discussion of personal problems. In these and other senses they can be companionable, supportive and helpful. It seems likely too that, to anticipate the next chapter, for most people with jobs what might be called the 'community' of work provides an important sense of identity.

We can, however, learn little about all this from British (or, for that matter, any other) studies in industrial sociology. What is certainly well-documented, as for example in a well-known enquiry in a Yorkshire mining village (Dennis et al., 1956), is the one-industry community in which workmates are often also relatives, neighbours, friends or all three. But this is a special case, since the links between the residential and work communities and their overlapping social networks are the distinctive characteristics of such districts, and the analysis of them throws no light on the relevance of work relationships in the more usual situation when the two worlds are separate.

There have of course been a number of studies of workplace relations, for example in garment and tailoring workshops (Lupton, 1963 and Cunnison, 1966), among managers and technical specialists (Sofer, 1970), on a car assembly line (Beynon, 1973), among women workers in a cigarette factory (Pollert, 1981) and in a hosiery workshop (Westwood, 1984). These studies were however mainly concerned with such issues as the effect of relationships upon output or the place of work in women's lives. They had little or nothing to say about the content and social relevance of the relationships. An analysis by Brown and his colleagues (1973) of the 'occupational culture' of ship-building workers comes closest to examining the meaning of 'friendship' at work, but even that does not go as deeply as might have been hoped.

In the absence of further evidence, I suggest that the main relevance of workplace relationships is at work, and that, though colleagues give each other advice and help (the help in particular usually being confined to work-related matters), social relationships between them are normally of major importance only when transformed into personal friendships which extend outside work. In the context of social care in particular work colleagues are best seen as constituting one source among others from which friends can be recruited. This was the view adopted in the discussion of 'work friends' in the chapter on friendship.

Much the same applies to relationships with people who are fellow members of a sports or social club, or pub drinking companions. Again, it would seem probable that in the main, though dealings with such people are normally 'friendly' (to use the slippery adjective once more) and though people met in this way no doubt sometimes give each other advice and help of minor kinds, the contacts are usually limited and relatively superficial, and become of serious relevance to the discussion of personal relationships and of informal care only if they develop further, outside the particular setting, into the general category of friendship. Given the absence of hard information, my concentration on the three main types of relationship is probably justified.

Self-help and voluntary organisations
Another gap in the discussion so far is about the contribution to social care by self-help groups and other voluntary bodies. Voluntary organisations vary widely in scale and structure, from large umbrella bodies like the National Council for Voluntary Organisations to the national and regional offices of Age Concern and then down to local children's playgroups and widows' clubs. Some of the voluntary sector provides no direct support or care for those needing help, examples being the National Trust, environmental bodies and pressure groups. But many other organisations do.

The Wolfenden Report noted that in the personal social services the contribution of the voluntary sector, including paid workers as well as volunteers, was greater than that of the statutory sector. The same report also usefully spelt out the role of the voluntary sector and its relationship to informal care.

There is widespread voluntary involvement in caring for the elderly, for children and for the handicapped. Some of this amounts to filling gaps in statutory provision, but much of it is different in kind from statutory provision, either because the beneficiaries are involved in mutual aid or because the voluntary helper can sometimes develop relationships not possible for paid professionals. In relation to the informal system of caring, the special contribution of the voluntary sector consists of filling or bridging the gaps between the individual and the statutory services, through the medium of organised arrangements for mutual aid and neighbourly care and by transmitting from one side to the other knowledge about unmet needs and available resources (Wolfenden Report, 1978).

To give an example of this kind of activity, most of the 'Good Neighbour' schemes of the kind studied by Philip Abrams are in the voluntary sector though a few are run by local authorities; all try to create bridges, in Wolfenden's phrase, between the formal and the informal - seeking to make fuller use of informal care by organising it rather more formally.

Self-help groups deserve separate attention. They are composed of people sharing a common problem or condition, examples being cancer, epilepsy, eczema, single-parenthood, widowhood, and having children with a particular disability. Though there are no reliable statistics (and hardly could be, given the difficulty of knowing what to include) the numbers of such groups have certainly increased in recent years: a recent directory listed over ten thousand in Britain (Mental Health Foundation, 1985). Such groups clearly help in meeting the needs of their members.

Another potential source of support is the church, chapel or other religious institution. Relatively few people in Britain attend or are active members: about one adult in five goes once a month or more and about half do not go at all except for weddings and funerals (National Opinion Polls, 1982). Likewise, few of those who might benefit are visited in their homes by ministers of religion. In Hunt's national survey of elderly people (1978), only one in six had been visited during the previous six months, though the proportion was found to be as high as a half in the study of elderly people in North Wales rural areas, where the chapel in particular exerts a strong influence in local life (Wenger, 1984).

Helpful though self-help groups, voluntary organisations and religious bodies are to some people - self-help groups to those with particular problems, for instance, and churches, chapels and the like in certain kinds of region, locality or ethnic group - their overall contribution to care is small compared with what is done by relatives, friends and neighbours. Philip Abrams, in his study of neighbouring and Good Neighbour schemes, asked a sample of 173 ordinary residents whom they would turn to for help with a particular problems, such as if a family member needed 'keeping an eye on' for a couple of weeks or 'looking after for a long time'. Not surprisingly, relatives predominated in the answers, with neighbours, then friends a long way behind. As Abrams explained:

> The categories 'church' and 'volunteers or voluntary organis- ations' do not appear ... because they were so rarely mentioned by respondents (Bulmer, 1986).

Thus the contribution made by these kinds of organisation is relatively unimportant in scale compared with the informal systems that are the main focus of this report.

Two qualifications should, however, be added. The first is that for minorities of people churches, workingmen's clubs and other voluntary bodies and groups do act as important sources of support, and self-help groups are particularly crucial in sustaining their members (Richardson and Goodman, 1983). Secondly, it would be a mistake to think of the voluntary sector as cut off from the informal. Not only do some parts of it deliberately seek to build links to informal carers. In addition, as noted in the Introduction, people who are first met in an institutional or semi- formal setting sometimes go on to become personal friends. Like the workplace and leisure settings mentioned earlier in this chapter, self-help groups, churches, social clubs and the like can be useful sources of personal relationships that develop and become supportive.

Kin, friends, neighbours: the distinctive roles

Now to the question of what it is that distinguishes the three main sources - kin, friends and neighbours. Some indications have already been given. These points are now brought together and developed, drawing on a range of further material, including an influential American article (Litwak and Szelenyi, 1969).

The origins of the kinship bond - biology, marriage or legal responsibility - mean that it is usually more enduring than other kinds of ties. A second feature is that, since relatives are often of different generations and (because of occupational mobility) in different social strata from each other, kin networks are usually heterogeneous in age and social class whereas friendship networks are often relatively homogeneous.

The relatives who are genealogically closest - parents, children and siblings - may also sometimes live near each other, as in the 'local extended families' described in Chapter II, and for them kinship can be a source of help of virtually all kinds. Among those living less close there are wide variations, depending on proximity and accessibility. Even when relatives do not live near, they can, and characteristically do, provide substantial support at critical times, for example with serious illness and infirmity. Despite the absence of frequent face to face meetings, with the aid of telephones and cars kin also arrange to help as required with, for example, transport, gardening, house maintenance and baby-sitting. Financial transfers - gifts or loans - can readily be made over any distance, and they are much more often made between kin, particularly across the generations, than between others.

As well as doing a wide range of other things, relatives and particularly women relatives carry the main burden of intensive and long-term care. Apart from the special case of spouses - who of course include men as well as women - it is female kin above all who do most of the nursing, washing and personal caring.

Despite what has been said earlier about the lack of formal rules in Western kinship, it seems that a strong sense of obligation survives in modern societies, with an expectation on the part of most people that relatives, especially close relatives, will make more effort to help than other people will or should. In other words, though there are no binding rules, there are apparently powerful norms.

Two further pressures may work in the same direction. The first is the general notion of reciprocity (which is another term for the notion of social exchange discussed in Chapter III). It is of course by no means true that it is because of an expectation of return that parents care for their dependent children, or brothers and sisters help each other. But it does seem plausible to suggest that an adult child feels some obligation to care for an aged parent partly because of an awareness of all the caring that in early life went in the opposite direction. Also one may be more willing to reciprocate in providing intimate personal care - and, perhaps more important, accepting it - when one has previously been on terms of close familiarity and intimacy during the years together in nuclear family. The years of dependence in the human species are long. And, just as long residence in the same locality seems to go hand in hand with an attachment to it and to the other people, so may the long years of shared living between parents and children encourage enduring attachment between them. In both neighbourhoods and kin groups familiarity encourages a sense of belonging.

Family relationships are entirely different from friendship, where the distinctive feature is personal choice. As the saying goes: 'You choose your friends but not your relatives'. The basis of friendship is a mixture of social exchange, affection and subsequent attachment. Friendship ties, like kinship ties, do not depend on proximity; they can likewise be maintained over distance, though the friendship needs to be emotionally close if the links are to overcome continuing practical difficulties in maintaining contact. Because friends are acquired among people sharing the same experience - in childhood, in education, at work, in leisure, rearing young children, living in the same locality - they are commonly broadly alike in age, income, education and social status. Friends are thus more likely than relatives to share similar cultural tastes, political opinions and views about 'modern' values and standards of behaviour.

Friends are leisure-time companions more often than relatives, particularly so among the young and single but also in later phases of the life-cycle. Friends are companions in sport and other leisure, sometimes go on holiday together, invite each other into their homes for drinks and meals. When it comes to support, close friends in particular often provide much reciprocal help. They lend or borrow their homes, cars and equipment, and they offer useful services, such as contacts in business or over jobs. They often advise over personal problems and provide sympathy and emotional support. Wenger (1984) argues that a range of research findings suggest that, despite the importance of relatives, 'friends assume a far greater importance where emotional and expressive backing is needed'. This is one of their distinctive roles.

They are, nevertheless, usually shown in research studies as relatively unimportant as sources of social care, particularly long-term personal care. Philip Abrams, writing more generally, said: 'Friends tend to be the weakest structurally of all primary groups in that they lack the permanence of the family and the frequent face-to-face contact of neighbours', adding that the evidence from his own study confirmed this view (Bulmer, 1986). This seems to go too far, bearing in mind the evidence, including for example that from my own studies in Woodford and Dagenham, where for young families with children in particular local friends at the same stage in life were major sources of day-to-day help with shopping, baby-sitting, child care and minor illnesses. The discrepancy may partly arise from the fact that Abrams, like some other researchers, was treating local friends as neighbours rather than (as I have done) a particular category of friends.

Neighbours themselves, by definition, live nearby and therefore are able to be in frequent face-to-face contact. Because most neighbours are relatively homogeneous in terms of income and class, they are often like each other in these respects, though less so than friends. They are more mixed than friends in age, but most people probably have more to do with those neighbours who are of similar age to themselves than with those much younger or older.

As far as help and care are concerned, the proximity of neighbours makes them particularly suitable for certain sorts of task. They mainly help in meeting day-to-day needs of fairly trivial kinds - feeding the cat, holding the keys, lending some sugar - but also in smaller or greater emergencies - a burst pipe, a fire, a sudden death. The distinctive contribution of neighbours as against others was described thus by Philip Abrams (in a passage which seems somewhat at variance with his remark just quoted about friends):

> Even neighbours on unfriendly terms would be likely to help each other out in emergencies or with local problems of a communal nature. But the long-term, arduous, time-consuming work of continuous care of an elderly or disabled person would be most unlikely to be undertaken by a neighbour unless there was added to neighbourliness some additional element such as friendship (Bulmer, 1986).

The main divisions of function between the three categories in terms of support and help are shown in Table V.1 (p.82). The division introduced earlier is again used, between people at the two main stages of life when help is needed. It can be assumed that for younger handicapped people, for example, the pattern would be much the same as is shown for the elderly, and that most of the kinds of help given to young families are also given to people at other stages in life.

In practice the division of labour is of course less clear-cut than the table suggests. There is some overlap of functions. There is sometimes also, as has been noted, some overlap between the categories. Two cousins of the same age may be friends as well as relatives. Neighbours often become friends and are even sometimes described as being like relatives, who are seen as 'closer' than friends. 'We're more like sisters than friends', as a Woodford woman said about a neighbouring woman of her own age (Willmott and Young, 1960).

The functions performed in particular cases depend not only on the relationship but also on other circumstances. As has already been said, when relatives live close at hand they usually also do the things neighbours typically do. Neighbours may then, in an emergency, be asked to act only as messenger: 'If I'm ill I knock on the wall and they go and get my sister' (Young and Willmott, 1957). The pattern of care is also influenced by the process of substitution - people stepping in when others are not available. If elderly people, for instance, have no children, then siblings may substitute; if no siblings, other relatives; and, if no relatives at all, friends or neighbours. There are, however, limits to the process: the substitution is not by any means complete, over the population as a whole. Elderly people without children - to continue the example - are in general less likely to receive informal care of any kind than those who have children, those without other relatives less likely than those with them, and so on.

Help can, of course, come from more than one source. Although there is usually one primary supporter - typically a daughter for an infirm elderly person, or the wife's mother or a local woman friend for a couple with young children - the different helpers often act in a complementary fashion. On the other hand, some may receive no help from any source. As Philip Abrams and his colleagues put it, specifically in terms of relatives and neighbours:

> ... help received from kin does not preclude help being received from neighbours; nor at the same time should we expect that low levels of family support will be accompanied by high levels of neighbourly help. Overall our preliminary findings indicate that there are in practice no necessary displacement or trade-off effects within the system of informal care between family and neighbours (Abrams et al., 1981).

The main conclusions are therefore as follows:

- Distinctive contributions are made by kin, friends, and neighbours, so there is some specialisation of functions between them.

- There is at the same time some capacity for substitution or compensation between the three categories.

There are, however, limits to this process. For most people, kin, friends, and neighbours offer complementary functions, meeting different kinds of need, rather than being used as alternatives.

In consequence, despite substitution, people without available kin, particularly close kin, are less likely to receive informal care than those who have them. This applies particularly to elderly people; younger families seem to be more able to create networks among their peers which are adequate in meeting most of their day-to-day needs, partly perhaps because the help they need is less demanding and more easily reciprocated.

Isolated people?

It is clear that the various potential sources of informal care do not, between them, necessarily provide people with either as much company or as much effective support as they need. The rest of this chapter looks at various kinds of people who might be likely to be worse off than others in terms of sociable contact and help. The evidence presented is highly variable and no attempt is made to be comprehensive. Some studies, for example, are based on large samples, others on small ones. And some studies go into detail, as others do not, about the care provided as distinct from social contacts.

Because of the growing number of very old people in the population the elderly are the biggest worry: those aged 85 and over in particular are expected to increase by a fifth in the next five years and nearly double in the next thirty. Several studies of elderly people use composite scores to identify the most isolated among them: the items include, for instance, living alone, having no close relatives, having no telephone and having no contact with neighbours. The Mark Abrams urban study in England in 1977, using an eighteen-point scale of isolation, found that no people aged 65 to 74 and only 1 per cent of those aged 75 or more were in the most isolated category (Abrams, 1978). The study in rural areas in North Wales in 1978-79 used a ten-point scale, on which 6 per cent of people were in the most isolated group (Wenger, 1984). In North Wales again, people aged 65 to 74 were less often isolated (4 per cent) than those aged 75 or over (10 per cent); people living alone were worse off than others (16 per cent in the highly isolated category), as were single people (20 per cent) and especially single men (29 per cent).

Such measures as these are not entirely satisfactory, not only because (as the examples show) different studies come up with different proportions but also because of the familiar problems of combining - and giving unitary weights to - diverse characteristics. A more intelligible measure of isolation, with the added advantage of a more recent national sample of over 4,000, is that used in a special analysis of the 1980 General Household Survey (Office of Population Censuses and Surveys, 1982). The survey found that about one in six of all elderly people saw relatives or friends less often than once a week. The proportion rose from one in eight among younger elderly people (65-69) to one in five among those aged 80 or over. Again it was higher among single people (a fifth) than others. It was lower among those who could drive and had a car (one in ten) and higher among those who were housebound (a quarter). Related to these last two findings, other evidence shows that the decline in contacts with age is due to a reduction in visits by elderly people to both relatives and friends (Hunt, 1978; Wenger, 1984).

The 1980 General Household Survey also asked about talking to neighbours. It found, to echo a point made earlier, that among those elderly people seeing relatives or friends at least once a week rather more talked to neighbours with the same frequency (83 per cent of them did so) than among those who saw relatives or friends less often (68 per cent). To him that hath, on the whole, shall be given - despite some substitution.

In all, the proportion of elderly people in the sample who did not speak to relatives, friends or neighbours as often as once a week - another, more extreme index of social isolation - was 5 per cent. People as cut off as this are unlikely to have ready access to informal care (though some will have relatives or friends living at a distance, who may be accessible and able to come in an emergency). As was explained in the chapter on kinship, those who lack social contacts are, not surprisingly, the kinds of people who depend most on the formal services (Sinclair et al., 1984).

Some studies have concentrated on the kinds of elderly people who are particularly likely to need care. Wenger followed up her initial general survey in North Wales by interviewing people aged 75 and over four years later. She found 'reassuring stability with evidence of family and personal adjustments taking place to accommodate changing needs'. She also noted, however, the some-times substantial 'pressures' on the informal carers (Wenger, 1984).

There have been several studies of elderly people with dementia, who amount to about one in 20 of those aged 65 or over and one in five of those aged 80 or over. At least four-fifths of them live in their own homes or those of relatives. Thus for most such people, informal care is provided though, again, often with strain upon the carers: 'Relatives are usually available, willing and able to make the key contribution, but they are generally worn down by the care they provide' (Levin et al., 1983).

Lone parents

Hunt's study (1973), which was drawn on earlier in describing the kinship contacts of married women, provides a comparison of these with the contacts of 'non-married' women and men with children. The research was in five local areas. It showed that non-married women had about as much contact with their parents as married women did. Non-married men had 'nearly as much contact' with parents as both sets of women if the parents were alive, but because the men were rather older fewer of them had parents alive. Previously-married women and men had, not surprisingly, less contact with their former parents-in-law, and the same applied with other relatives of their former spouse. What is more, the lone mothers and fathers had often lost contact with their own relatives other than parents.

As for contacts with friends, much smaller proportions of lone mothers than married received visits from, or made visits to, friends. The proportions were even lower among lone fathers. No information was collected about neighbours in Hunt's survey, but some is available from the MORI survey already referred to. This found that the proportion of lone parents who spoke to neighbours was similar to that among people from other kinds of family, and that lone parents visited neighbours and were visited by them rather more often than others. As reported in the previous chapter, they also gave and received more help. So the general picture is a mixed one: lone parents seem more isolated than married people in some respects but not in others.

Prisoners' wives

A particular category of lone wives, many with dependent children, is women whose husbands are in prison. The only available information about such wives comes from a national survey in the early 1960s, in which nearly 600 were interviewed (Morris, 1965).

The survey found that over a quarter of the wives had moved following their husbands' conviction, about half of them having gone to live with their own parents. In general relatives were seen more often than previously, and they were the main source of informal help. Over a third of those not living with relatives received 'material help' from kin, and wives received 'much more active support from their own parents than from in-laws, friends and neighbours'.

Relationships with parents were not, however, always harmonious. Such relationships were assessed as 'sympathetic and helpful' by 62 per cent of the wives. Comparable percentages for others were: siblings, 69 per cent; in-laws, 45 per cent; friends, 73 per cent; and neighbours, 60 per cent.

The apparently high percentages among friends is misleading, because those who had not remained sympathetic were often excluded, being no longer either met or regarded as friends. In general, as with relatives, those friends who remained were visited more frequently than before the husband's conviction.

As for neighbours, their hostility was 'far more wounding than similar attitudes from others ... neighbours are, by definition, there all the time, so the influence they have on your day-to-day life is in some respects greater than that of relatives and friends' (Morris, 1966). One wife in 20 reported 'hostility in the community' as among their problems. Stresses of this kind were often given as a reason for having moved away from the previous home. Nevertheless, Morris reported that, no doubt because of their isolation, in general wives spent more time talking to neighbours than they had done in the past.

Thus the fact of their husbands going to prison caused some problems in the wives' social relationships. Most were, however, not isolated as a result, though they must have been worse off in other ways. Friends who had remained loyal provided companionship, as did neighbours for most, though presumably at a superficial level. The main finding was the overwhelming importance of relatives, particularly the wife's parents, in providing support.

Physical and mental handicap

A review of informal care by Parker (1985) concluded that most adults with physical disabilities or chronic illnesses were cared for informally, and mainly by relatives. The conclusions were less cheering, however, for mentally handicapped adults or for the parents of severely disabled children.

A study was carried out of all the people with mental handicap registered with the Sheffield Mental Health Service in 1968 (Bayley, 1973). A third of those with severe mental handicap were then in hospitals or residential homes; the proportion is likely to be smaller now. But, among those who were living at home, the extent of informal support from outside the household was not always substantial. Bayley reported that of the available siblings, three-quarters gave 'much' or 'average' help, leaving a quarter who gave 'very little' or 'none'. Among outside relatives generally the proportion helping was somewhat lower. Those families not getting help often explained this on grounds of the relatives' infirmity or distance, and Bayley noted that one weakness of the research was that the availability of kin was not systematically recorded. It is, however, clear that some carers were bitter that they received so little support: 'I don't get any help at all'; 'They never bother, not a bit of help, no'. The importance of propinquity showed up when the contribution of neighbours was considered. Neighbours, including 'neighbours who had become friends', helped as often as siblings did.

Overall, Bayley assessed that the extent of informal support was 'good' for just over half the families, 'shaky' for a fifth and 'poor' for a quarter. The main reasons given for the absence of help, apart from availability, were to do with people's own attitudes. Bayley reported that some families 'wanted to hide away the pain of their sub-normal member', and others showed 'a reluctance to intrude on other people'; as he said, the two attitudes might well be related to each other.

Two more recent studies, both of families in which there were handicapped children, likewise suggest that when such people have similarly severe and continuing family burdens relatives, although in touch socially, may again not be very effective in providing care of the continuing or 'tending' kind. Wilkin (1979) concluded, from a survey of 120 families with severely mentally handicapped children:

> Many of the families had a high level of contact with kin and there was often some sort of mutual supportive relationship ... (But) support from the kinship network was not usually relevant to the day-to-day domestic routine.

The same was noted by Glendinning (1983) in an intensive study of 17 families with a disabled child. She found that 'none of the families studied had regular or frequent practical help' from relatives outside the household. Like Bayley, she suggested that, though this was partly for practical reasons - distance or relatives' own family commitments - there was also a reluctance on the part of some families with handicapped children to seek such help even from kin.

Both studies reported that non-relatives also did little. Glendinning said that practical help from neighbours was limited and Wilkin that 'Friends provided even less support in day-to-day routine than did relatives'. More generally, he concluded that his research 'cast considerable doubt' on the contribution of social networks to 'the daily routine of childcare and housework' for such families.

One other study, however, of the families of children with cystic fibrosis in Northern Ireland, found a good deal of support from relatives and other local people. Nine out of ten had substantial support from relatives, and half had occasional help from neighbours (Burton, 1975). The discrepancy is puzzling. Parker (1985) suggests that the explanation is that expectations and norms vary substantially from one type of 'community' to another, a point that is taken up in the next chapter. The general picture is, however, clear: families with children or other members who suffer severe mental or physical handicap may not be socially isolated, but they are likely to lack informal support of a substained kind from outside the household.

Unemployment

The unemployed are the final group whose special circumstances might affect their informal social relationships and the help they receive from informal sources. On the first of these questions, some effects are obvious enough. Mention was made earlier in this chapter of the role of relationships with work colleagues and of the shared sense of community at work. When people lose their job they lose these 'social' advantages of working. If we knew more about social life at work we could talk more confidently about the degree of loss for people in different kinds of occupation, but even as it is some such loss seems likely to be common as one of the social costs of unemployment.

Likewise, unemployed people are less likely to go out - to pubs, cinemas and so on - than people with jobs. In Michael White's national sample survey of 3,000 unemployed men and women, in 1980 and 1981, one unemployed person in every six said they had given up 'going out socially' during the previous year (White, forthcoming). In another national survey, of 1,000 unemployed people in 1982, over half said they had 'cut back on leisure or spare time activities', and 'going out socially' was among the activities most frequently mentioned (Economist Intelligence Unit, 1982). And a sample survey of 1,700 people in Bristol in 1979 found that only two-thirds of unemployed people, compared with four-fifths of those in work, had 'been out socially for an evening' during the month before the interview (Mitton et al., 1983). So in this sense people's social life seems to have suffered as a result of the loss of their job.

This does not necessarily mean social contact with relatives and friends falls off with unemployment. White asked people whether they saw existing friends more or less often than they had a year earlier, and also whether they had made any new friends. Between a quarter and a third said they saw their friends less often than previously, but a similar proportion said they had made new friends.

The Bristol survey compared the 162 unemployed people with the 1532 who were under retirement age and in jobs; all were asked about their most recent contacts with relatives and friends. In terms of relatives there was no marked difference between the unemployed and the others. The figures on friends suggested that the unemployed had rather fewer contacts with them, but the differences were not marked. In the Economist Intelligence Unit survey of 1,000 unemployed people 28 per cent said that their 'group of friends' had changed as a result of unemployment; the proportion was higher - 39 per cent - among people who had been unemployed for more than two years. Among those reported changes the main ones were as follows: lack of money restricted contacts with regular friends, they had fewer friends, they had lost touch with old friends or former workmates, and - on the more positive side - they had made new friends who were themselves unemployed. The 72 per cent whose group of friends had not changed were asked whether they saw them as frequently or less frequently than before. About half said they saw friends as frequently as before, the others dividing fairly evenly between those with more frequent and those with less frequent contacts; a larger proportion of younger people than older said they saw their friends more frequently than before.

In another survey in 1982 a total of 1,150 registered unemployed 17-year-olds living in urban areas in England were interviewed. They were disadvantaged young people in the sense that they had left school at the minimum leaving age and had limited educational qualifications; about a third were black. They were asked about the young people with whom they spent their time during the evenings and weekends. It turned out that these other people were often also unemployed, and this was particularly true of the young unemployed blacks (Banks et al., 1984).

White's national survey provides some answer to the question of the help that unemployed people receive from others. Just over a third said they had been helped by relatives with money or in kind and another fifth with other forms of aid. Friends, yet again, less often provided it. Fewer than one unemployed person in ten had been helped by friends with cash or in kind, and a similar low proportion had received other help from them.

On the evidence of these various studies, therefore, people continue to see their relatives, as one would expect. As for friends, they may lose touch with some but also make some others, with little overall effect on their contacts. For unemployed people, unlike those in the other minority groups examined, the conclusion seems to be that social relationships do not markedly change. On the positive side, relatives and, to a lesser extent, friends act as informal sources of help with the problems, particularly financial, that unemployed people face. But the limitations of these studies are plain.

Conclusion

This chapter has shown how relatives, friends and neighbours play different roles as informal associates and make their own distinctive contributions in help and support. It also shows, however, that despite a process of partial substitution, there are important gaps. There are minorities who are socially isolated. There are others who need personal care on a continuing basis and do not receive enough. These include some of the very elderly and in particular confused elderly people, together with families which have mentally handicapped and severely physically handicapped children and adults. Some of the carers of such people, lacking enough outside support, are themselves under strain.

The policy issues raised by these findings are taken up in the final chapter. Before that, however, informal relationships are viewed from a different perspective - that of the role of the local community.

Table V.1 Forms of help from relatives, friends and neighbours to young families and elderly people

	Relatives	Friends	Neighbours
Young families	Financial help/ advice Help at child-birth Help with the care of young children e.g in serious illness Support in personal/ matrimonial difficulties	Day-to-day help with e.g. young children/shopping/ home maintenance (local friends) Emotional support Advice Contacts	Minor services with e.g. pets/keys/loans of food or tools/ home maintenance/ gardening Emergency help e.g. fire/sudden illness/ sudden death
Elderly people	Care in infirmity Transport Social visiting	Emotional support Advice Contacts Transport Social visiting	'Surveillance' Minor services (as for young) Emergency help (as for young)

In examining the relevance and characteristics of neighbourhood and community in complex modern societies such as Britain, the first hurdle is again the terminology. 'Neighbourhood' in itself poses fewer problems; it refers to a local residential area, the only immediate semantic question being about the scale being referred to. 'Community' presents more difficulty.

The central notion is that people (or occasionally other things) have something in common. In the most general usage, what people share is just residence in a given area: the territory or place.   A second sense refers to people having in common something other than place, examples of such groupings of people being the Jewish community and the scientific community. This is often labelled a community of interest - or interest community - it being accepted that 'interest' is broadly interpreted to cover shared characteristics as diverse as ethnic origin, religion, politics, occupation, leisure pursuit and sexual propensity.   A further example discussed earlier is the self-help or mutual aid group composed of people who share a common condition or problem. Another way of describing any of these interest communities is as examples of social networks: the idea of a net is particularly appropriate here because it can be readily seen that the members are linked up not to everybody but only to those sharing the same interest or characteristic.

The two concepts of place community and interest community are not mutually exclusive. They can overlap in the sense that, although interest communities are often geographically dispersed, they can also exist inside even quite small areas. Thus, within a person's neighbourhood, his or her social relationships may be dominated by fellow-members of a local interest community such as a church, an ethnic group or a political party.

These first two meanings refer merely to collections of people; a local place community, for example, is simply the population of a particular geographical area. But in common usage community does not necessarily refer just to the fact of people living in the same place or sharing the same interests. It refers also to a meaning which is at least as important as the other two - is indeed in one sense the essence of the word, as it is commonly used - but is more elusive and often has rhetorical or moral overtones absent with the first two meanings. In this application, the concern is with people's feelings, and also with the patterns of relationships that reflect, sustain and encourage those feelings. Terms such as 'sense of community' and 'spirit of community' suggest the central idea.

Whatever term is used, the question is whether or rather to what extent a particular territorial community or interest community is the third kind of community as well. Particular places (to take the territorial example) are this kind of community to a greater or lesser degree, and the question is how much. In practice, the degree is essentially a reflection of the proportion of people for whom it is this kind of community.

It is not easy to select a label for this third meaning. One problem is that, as already indicated, it contains two elements. One is to do with social relationships: a place is more of this kind of community if many residents know many others. The second element is to do with perceptions, with how many people feel a sense of identity with the place and of solidarity with the other people.

The two elements - interaction with others and a sense of identity - usually go together, because they reinforce each other. The point was demonstrated in a reanalysis (Janowitz and Kasarda, 1974) of a national survey done in 1967. In the original study (known as the 'community attitudes survey') a representative sample of 2000 electors in England (excluding Greater London) had been asked various questions about local community attachment and about social relationships and participation. The authors concluded from their reanalysis:

> ... we have shown that community sentiments were substantially influenced by participation in social networks. Whether or not a person experienced a sense of community, had a strong interest in the affairs of the community, or would be sorry to leave the community was found to be strongly influenced by his local friendship and kinship bonds and formal and informal associational ties.

In other words, the two aspects are, as one would assume, closely interrelated. It should be noted that the original survey was done nearly twenty years ago, and one cannot be sure that if it were repeated so large a proportion would now feel a sense of attachment to their local territorial community (nearly four in five did so at that date) or that the same relationship would hold between local ties and community sense. But in trying to make sense of the terminology without becoming over-complicated, it seems reasonable to assume (as I have done so far) that the two elements are in effect parts of the same thing.

But what should that be called? I propose to use the term 'community of attachment' for it, alongside territorial community and interest community. The advantage of the word 'attachment' is that it combines both meanings, suggesting attachment to people (in and through relationships with them) and to place. The particular term is, however, not important in itself. It is intended merely as form of shorthand, to indicate the presence of absence (or, again, the extent) of the two crucial extra characteristics - interaction with others and sense of identity - that distinguish this notion from those of territory and interest. It should be emphasised that both territorial and interest communities can exhibit the characteristics of the community of attachment and the degree to which they do so in practice is one of the central questions for the chapter.

Geographical scale
In considering the present role and function of neighbourhood and community, a crucial distinction is that between local communities and non-local ones (the latter being interest communities which are geographically dispersed). But a key question is the one about scale: how local is local?

This cannot be answered in precise terms, for example by specifing a population of a particular size. For one thing most people, reflecting the reality of the matter, seem to think in terms of a hierarchy of scales. The most local level corresponds to a person's own street or block of flats and one or two adjacent ones. We found this to be the most relevant scale in terms of local community in the Bethnal Green of the 1950s. We called it the 'precinct' and, leaving aside the current American connotation, that seems as good a term for it as any other. The population of such an area is seldom more than a few hundred.

Most residents have some notion of a larger neighbourhood or community as well - a local area containing several thousand people - and some go further afield, instead or additionally, to an area with a much larger population. Others again distinguish local areas primarily in terms of functions that make sense to them, examples being the area within which they can easily walk with very young children, the catchment of a local primary school (because the children's schoolfriends, and the parents of those schoolfriends, are drawn from that area) or, depending on their affiliations, the church parish or political ward.

These examples indicate that, as there is bound to be with the area immediately around the home (each home being, as it were, the centre of a different map), there is a good deal of divergence from person to person about the boundaries of wider neighbourhoods as perceived by them. There are also differences in the size of such subjectively perceived neighbourhoods. Both kinds of variation are apparent in studies in which people have been asked to identify the boundaries (Lee, 1968; Hampton, 1970; Baker and Young, 1971). These studies also show, however, that there is usually some degree of consensus. On size, most researchers have found that the majority of people think in terms of areas smaller than wards, with populations of up to 5000 or so (Royal Commission on Local Government in England, 1969). And, despite the individual variations in boundaries, certain physical frontiers are commonly identified by residents of particular districts. For example, in surveys in Northampton and Ipswich (Willmott, 1967) such frontiers included major roads, railway lines and rivers. Awareness of the importance of physical markers has led to their deliberate use in the planning of new towns in order to create recognisable neighbourhood units there.

If it is sensible to think of two or more tiers of neighbourhood, how do these then relate to the concept of community, and of local community in particular? It is clear that community is a generic term, and that territorial communities exist at a variety of scales, going up from a few streets, a city, and a nation, even up to a group of nations (as with the European Community). As some of the earlier discussion has illustrated, communities at the smaller geographical scales are often described as neighbourhoods: neighbourhood is a synonym for community at the most local level.

Unless one stretches the word local beyond its reasonable meaning, the term local community cannot normally be applied above the scale of a town or, within a large city, to what is in local government terms a district or borough. A suggested hierarchy of local communities is in Table VI.1 (p.102). The table refers to urban areas, where most of Britain's population live; a comparable scheme could be drawn for rural areas. It should be recognised that the hierarchy is intended only as a broad indication and that, as explained, there can be other tiers than those shown, both in people's perceptions and for particular functional purposes. It is also accepted that there are certain senses in which cities as large as Birmingham, Newcastle-upon-Tyne and even London are seen as, and function as, territorial communities in the lives of their residents. Londoners, for instance, often feel some sense of identity with the metropolis as a whole, and some affection for it. Such large areas are, however, excluded here on the grounds that they are above the size that could properly be recognised as local, being a further step up the ladder of scales leading to a region, the country and beyond.

Dispersed communities

Modern communications, and the greater residential and personal mobility they have made possible, have encouraged the development of dispersed communities - or networks - at the expense of local ones. People increasingly interact with others who do not share residence with them at any of the local levels just described. In many respects, these developments represent greater choice and variety in people's lives: greater choice over where to live, where to work and whom to mix with; greater variety because specialised interests and tastes can more readily be accommodated within the larger catchment areas (and larger populations) now accessible than they could in the limited territorial communities of the past. These are among the benefits of modern 'communities without propinquity' (Webber, 1964).

But how important are these dispersed communities and how far do they operate as communities of attachment? In answering this question, a distinction has to be made between dispersed communities of relatives or friends on the one hand, and of those less intimate on the other. (To apply the term community to a network of friends or kin may seem to stretch it too far, but it makes sense in the context of the broader discussion.)

As the research reported earlier has confirmed, today relatives and friends do not necessarily live near each other. On the contrary, most people now belong to kinship and friendship networks that are of susbstantial importance in their social lives but are geographically dispersed. But with modern transport and particularly the private car, with telephones, with enough space to have relatives or friends to stay for weekends or holidays, such dispersed communities can and often do operate effectively, and this includes the provision of help.

Members of dispersed extended families in particular not only maintain contact with each other but also have a sense of family identity. To some extent the same thing apply to larger kin networks (that is, including more distant relatives such as cousins and aunts). Certain circles of friends, too, keep in touch and are aware of their common membership, particularly when a group of them have known each other for a long time. Links with friends, even if close, are however more often in the form of loose-knit networks, in which most of one's various friends seldom meet each other, and in which there is usually little or no sense of collective identity.

The two main elements of the community of attachment - interaction and sense of identity - can operate in wider circles than just those people with whom one has relationships of a personal kind. The importance of these contacts with others, even if trivial, and of the sense of identity should not be underestimated. If people see themselves as sharing membership with others - whether work colleagues, or people with similar beliefs, political convictions or problems - this helps them, even in the absence of personal relationships, to locate themselves in the wider social structure, and to make sense of their lives in what may otherwise seem a complex and anonymous world.

Less personal kinds of dispersed interest community obviously vary in the extent to which they are also communities of attachment. Work communities often seem to be fairly strongly so. They are of course unusual in that most of them are 'local' when colleagues are at work even though 'dispersed' in terms of their homes and residential areas. As well as personal friendships made at work, relationships with co-workers seem to constitute for most people an important basis of common membership and identity. They are witness to the reinforcement that regular face-to-face contact brings to all human relationships.

Self-help groups too, even when geographically dispersed, often have fairly regular contacts and a strong community sense, derived from the shared recognition of a shared problem and shared efforts to do something about it. There are also other kinds of dispersed community marked by interaction and community sense, examples being those where the basis is a strongly felt religious, political or campaigning set of beliefs and objectives.

But most of the other dispersed interest communities in which people participate are fairly loose groupings. Their membership changes often, people's levels of participation fluctuate, and the reinforcement of continuing contact is lacking. These groupings are, like most circles of people's friends, more often loose-knit networks rather than communities of attachment. Examples are an adult education class in photography, and a group who come together to play or watch a sport.

The variations between dispersed communities are thus explained by differences in their basis and function, and by the strength of personal ties and shared benefits.

Local communities

The key question about the local community concerns the extent to which it is something more than just a place, the two criteria again being social interaction and community sense. Even superficial interaction has a bearing on how people feel about their locality. As the report of an ethnographic survey in Battersea, London, explained :

> Regular residents ... inevitably get to know each other by sight. They meet shopping, standing at the bus-stop or walking in the street, and so learn, over time, the public habits and timetables of people they do not know by name and probably never visit at home. Recognising and being recognised by others creates a sense of belonging (Wallman, 1984).

The material presented in earlier chapters makes it plain that the bulk of the population, as well as having such knowledge of other residents, have social relationships with people who live nearby. A sizeable minority have relatives living close at hand, most have some friends within ten minutes' walk of their home, and the overwhelming majority have friendly dealings with their neighbours. So, even in the absence of other evidence, it would certainly be wrong to suggest, as for example Clarke (1982) has, that the local territorial community now has virtually no role.

Some trends are, however, working against the locality, and some of these, such as residential mobility and increased car ownership, have already been mentioned as promoting dispersal. Another influence was the post-war programme of clearance and redevelopment in Britain's towns and cities; this not only broke up existing local networks but also redeveloped the old districts in physical forms which made it difficult for people to get to know their new neighbours. Yet another factor has been the post-war rise in the number and proportion of wives working outside the home; although to some extent this change has been made possible by the support of relatives and friends, who often help in caring for children, the general effect must have been to reduce contacts with people living nearby.

What is more, when men and women are not at work they now spend more time inside their homes than in the past. Their lives are more 'privatised' (Goldthorpe et al., 1969). This trend has been encouraged by improvements in housing standards, spaciousness and household appliances, and in particular the 'miniaturisation' of equipment (Young and Willmott, 1973), including washing machines, television, videos and the like. The growth in home-centredness has tended increasingly to polarise people's lives between the home on the one hand and places distant from it on the other.

Local ties and local institutions, however, continue to endure, and several counter-trends are working to strengthen their role. One such change is demographic: the increasing proportion in the population of older people who are more likely to spend time in the locality. They are being joined by others in the present economic climate, because of unemployment, job-sharing, early retirement and shorter working hours. Even the home-centredness just mentioned is, in its latest phase, likely to increase rather than reduce activity within the local area. A range of technological developments - home computers, word processors, links via optical fibres to commercial services, data banks and information networks - are opening the way to a regeneration of cottage industry in new forms. Meanwhile, changes in the relationships between the sexes are reinforcing the switch to the home as a place of paid work. Although most of the time of the new homeworkers will inevitably be spent inside the homes, they are likely to be more in evidence in the locality than if they worked elsewhere.

Variations in local community
As has been suggested in earlier chapters, the effects of these trends and counter-trends have not been uniform. Places vary in the number and strength of local ties and in the degree of local identity or community sense. Patterns differ, too, for different kinds of people, even in the same places.

What are the characteristics of place that influence the extent of local inter-relationships and local identity? First, the negative findings. The reanalysis of the 1967 community attitudes survey found that neither urban scale nor population density affected the extent of local social networks or community sense (Janowitz and Kasarda, 1974). Thus it is not true, as is often asserted, that communities of attachment are rarer in large cities than in small towns.

On the positive side, the same analysis showed people's length of residence in an area to be the main factor:

The longer the length of residence, the more extensive were friendship and kinship bonds and local associational ties (Janowitz and Kasarda, 1974).

90

Despite the undoubted influence of long residence, however, other research has shown that it is possible for neighbourly relationships and sentiments to develop without it. Examples are studies in the United States (Whyte, 1957) and Britain (Willmott and Young, 1960) of middle-class suburbs where most people were relatively new, but in which newcomers were welcomed and themselves had the capacity to make local friends quickly - places where residents had the necessary aptitudes or social skills. Litwak and Szelenyi have pointed out (1969) that neighbourliness develops more quickly in a changing local population if people share a readiness to be friendly and helpful, and argue that such attitudes are becoming more widespread.

So the effects of newness in a district can be mitigated, though this does not undermine the general conclusion. Local kinship likewise helps to encourage community attachment, and of course is closely related to long residence: a settled area where many people have lived for much of their lives is almost bound also to be a place with a high proportion of local kinship ties. Similarly, having kin in the locality helps in itself to promote social relationships and a sense of local identity.

Klein (1965), in her review of the community studies of the 1950s, went further, arguing that 'kin living in the neighbourhood rather than unrelated neighbours are mainly responsible for neighbourliness', and Philip Abrams repeated the point later (1980). Clearly, kinship is an important element in what Abrams called the 'traditional community' (a term to which I return later), but its influence cannot easily be disentangled, just because it is usually so mixed up with long residence.

The combination shows the power of 'overlapping ties' (Fischer, 1977). Another example is where there is a concentration of fellow-residents with the same ethnic background in a neighbourhood, as with Asians in Small Heath, Birmingham and West Indians in Brixton, London. Yet another is where a majority of local people work in the same industry, illustrated in the Liverpool dock area studied by Kerr (1958) and the Yorkshire mining town examined by Dennis and his colleagues (1956).

As well as such overlapping ties, Fischer also cites two other sets of circumstances which are propitious. One is physical isolation, for example in remote rural areas or 'among carless suburban housewives'; being isolated, such people are dependent on each other for companionship and identity. The other influence mentioned by Fischer is 'an external threat'. It has become increasingly common in Britain in the 1970s and 1980s (as in the United States from about the 1950s) for local residents to join together in fighting what are seen as outside dangers. Examples are campaigns for local bypasses, against - or for - local traffic management schemes, and against the closure of schools or hospitals. The local organisation set up to campaign often continues in existence, pursuing local interests in other matters as they come up. And clearly, despite the formality or quasi-formality of the organisation, it can also help to develop informal relationships between local people along with a greater sense of local identity.

Physical form is yet another influence. Certain kinds of layout can be more conducive than others to neighbourly contact and identity (Kuper, 1953; Hole, 1959; Willmott, 1963; Newman, 1973). In particular, the large estates of council flats, often high-rise, which are such a distinctive feature in post-war redevelopment schemes in British cities have proved to be generally discouraging to sociability between neighbours (Willmott and Cooney, 1963; Coleman, 1985).

The physical form, together with the relative newness and the absence of longstanding ties, help to explain the dramatic changes in social relationships in the inner areas of British cities and older towns since the mid-1950s. Studies around that date and earlier had portrayed such places as 'urban villages' with 'widespread kindship ties and deeply-rooted neighbour relationships' (Jennings, 1962). Jennings was writing about an inner area of Bristol; she could just as well have been referring to Bethnal Green in the 1950s or to one of a dozen places, including Wolverhampton (Sheldon, 1948), inner Oxford (Mogey, 1956) and the Liverpool dock area just mentioned (Kerr, 1958). But by the the 1970s, as officially-sponsored inner area studies concluded, redevelopment and the dispersal of population had encouraged changes in the social character of such places. The study in Small Heath, Birmingham reported, for example:

> Kin relationships no longer seem to provide a bridge to the wider community or between generations in Small Heath ... Redevelopment has undermined relations with neighbours, first through the demolition of terraces with long-established populations, second because it has created temporary communities with especially high levels of mutual jealousy and conflict, and third because of the destruction of clubs, shops and churches (Llewelyn-Davies et al., 1977).

Subsequent research suggests that inner areas are now more often characterised by social isolation and conflict than by neighbourliness (Knight and Hayes, 1981; Harrison, 1983). But even in such areas, some people have kin or friends nearby and some find the social atmosphere congenial. This is partly a question of the type of housing - and the character of the particular precinct - in which they live. A study in Southwark, London in 1975 found that people in council housing, and those in high flats in particular, were more disposed than others to say that there was 'no community' in their area (Prescott-Clarke and Hedges, 1976).

Attitudes are also influenced by ethnic background and the social ties that go with it. Both the Birmingham and Lambeth inner area studies reported that those who were now most linked to kin and friends in their districts, and who felt most attached to the places, were the ethnic minorities - Asians in Birmingham and West Indians in Lambeth - whose local attachment has been referred to earlier.

Some researchers have suggested, on the basis of studies in suburban council estates, that they too are relatively lacking in community sense and local networks: this was the conclusion drawn by Klein (1965) from her review. But the study of the 'cottage estate' at Dagenham forty years after it had been built showed that there something like the traditional East End style of attachment community had eventually grown up, and therefore suggested that the newness, rather than other characteristics, was the main explanation for the initial coolness among residents (Willmott, 1963). As Klein herself pointed out, however, the circumstances in the 1950s and 1960s, as now, were different from those in which the first generation settled at Dagenham in the 1920s and 1930s. Without further evidence - from post-1945 estates a generation on - it is not possible to say to what extent the old forms of kinship and local community have been re-established.

Social class and local community

Council estates, like many inner areas, have predominantly working-class populations, whereas most suburban areas are middle-class or at least more mixed. What influence does social class have on local communities?

First, it seems that, contrary to the common impression, a mixture of classes in a neighbourhood tends to work against the development of community ties and sentiments, which flourish more in a homogeneous setting. Writing about the country town of Banbury in the 1950s, Stacey reported that 'mixture of classes within a street or neighbourhood appears to reduce the frequency and intensity of neighbourly contact and support' (Stacey, 1960).

The influence upon community ties of class itself, as distinct from the mix, is more difficult to determine. The Bethnal Green of the 1950s, as a traditional working-class area, is often seen as the epitome of local community. Yet when we compared it with middle-class Woodford, the contrast was by no means as sharp as expected. Certainly, the forms were different: there was less overt public 'matiness' in the suburb and fewer people there had the fierce local pride that was near-universal in Bethnal Green. But virtually every suburbanite had a network of local friends and most had some sense of community identity. In the way referred to earlier, many people had been ready to approach others and make friends nearby, thus overcoming the apparent handicaps to their newness to the district.

They had often joined local organisations, from tennis clubs to dramatic societies, from church groups to residents' associations, and had got to know others in that way. In general, ties through formal organisations 'foster more extensive primary contacts within the local community', and these contacts in their turn encourage a sense of community (Janowitz and Kasarda, 1974). Middle-class people are more enthusiastic joiners - the London Region survey in 1970 found membership of clubs or organisations twice as high among professional and managerial people as among semi-skilled and unskilled manual workers - and this is therefore another way in which such people compensate for their relative newness. Indeed, in one sense they are often more involved and active in their local community. The reanalysis of the 1967 national survey of community attitudes showed that 'higher social status produces greater interest in community affairs, both directly and indirectly, through more extensive and expanded formal associational ties ... higher status people have the skills and tastes required for such associational involvement' (Janowitz and Kasarda, 1974).

One interpretation of all this is that, contrary to the earlier belief, middle-class areas are now more neighbourly than traditional working-class ones. This is exactly what Philip Abrams argued on the basis of his study of ten areas with neighbourhood care schemes:

The comparison of social classes suggests an inversion of the traditional sociological stereotypes of the close-knit, highly integrated working-class community and the atomised, privatised domestic world of the middle-classes. The study provides evidence of the demise of traditional neighbourly working-class communities ... It is now in working-class neighbourhoods that people are more likely to keep themselves to themselves ... There is more evidence of organised neighbourliness in middle-class areas, albeit somewhat more formalised but nevertheless ... a potentially important source of social contact (Bulmer, 1986).

Abrams went too far here in suggesting that the traditional working-class community is now extinct - as I show later he himself found examples of it in the same study - and was almost certainly exaggerating the transformation. But the body of evidence on local relationships does suggest that, whereas in the past community attachment was particularly strong among working-class residents, it may now be, if anything, rather stronger among middle-class. This is, of course, in general terms; as some of the examples show, the detailed picture varies from place to place.

Variations between people
Another way to look at the differences in local communities is in terms of the circumstances and needs of different kinds of people, because this has a bearing on the importance to them of their neighbourhood.
First, the mothers of young children - and those children themselves - usually spend more time in the locality than other people; they therefore have more local contacts and more often exchange neighbourly help. In general, they are more fully members of the local social community than at other stages in life. If the mothers have jobs or private transport or both, this is less likely to be true. Elderly people are, because of restricted mobility, another category who depend largely on local contacts, again particularly if they are without private transport. In most districts the numbers of these sets of people are not negligible. Children aged ten or under and their mothers, together with people aged 70 or over, account for nearly a third of Britain's total population. As suggested in Chapter IV, people's family background and personal experience are also likely to affect the extent of their local attachment. Some researchers have also tried to distinguish between personality types in explaining variations. Kuper (1953), for example, drew a distinction between people who were 'reserved' and those who were 'sociable', which may to some extent reflect the distinction between 'rough' and 'respectable' families, so often observed on council estates. But these are rather imprecise notions and it is not possible to say much about them or about the relative weight to be attributed to them.

Attachment and locality: an assessment

To sum up this discussion of the various kinds of influences at work, territorial communities are likely to be attachment communities - to a greater rather than a lesser extent - under the following conditions:

- When there has been relative population stability, and thus large proportions of people have had lengthy continuous residence in the area.

- When kin live in the area.

- When many people work in a local industry.

- When people are alike in social class and income, or share membership of a particular ethnic minority.

- When a place is particularly isolated.

- When physical layout and design encourage rather than discourage casual neighbourly meetings and a sense of separate physical identity.

- When a large proportion of local people have the social skills, and the appropriate values, to get to know others quickly.

- When there are many locally-based organisations.

- When a place is under an external threat, particularly when this results in the creation of local campaigning organisations (though this may be a more temporary effect then the others).

In terms of the people, the following more often develop local attachments:

- Those, again, who have the appropriate skills and values including a readiness to join local organisation - all of which have so far been more common among middle-class people.

- Those who have young children (especially if the mother is not in full-time work outside the home and has no car) and those who are elderly (again, especially if they have no car).

-    Those whose family background, past experience or temperament predispose them to be sociable.

Many of the characteristics in these lists fall into one or other of two distinct categories, the others being 'neutral' in these terms. The first set might be described as the 'traditional' bases of solidarity and local interaction: long residence, having kin locally and being relatively constrained by the lack of private transport. These characteristics have been more common in working-class districts than others. They are the ones which, without deliberate effort from residents, help to encourage the growth of local relationships and loyalties.

The second set by contrast depends on the disposition and action of people themselves: the application of social skills in making friends nearby, and the readiness to do so; the creation of local campaigns against actual or potential external threats; the existence of many local organisations. Such means, it is clear, have in the past been more often used by middle-class people, and have therefore been more important in middle-class areas than others.

In assessing how local community stands in the 1980s, this distinction - based on the modes by which communities of attachment are developed - provides a useful starting point. Each mode corresponds to a distinctive style of attachment community - the traditional and the non-traditional - and an obvious question is about the relative importance of each. There are in this two-fold distinction some affinities to that made by Philip Abrams (and already referred to) between what he called, respectively, the traditional community (or neighbourhood) and new neighbourhoodism. He described the first in terms familiar to those who know the post-war community studies.

We probably all have a fairly definite idea of what the traditional neighbourhood was like. There are also enough pieces of fairly strong social and historical research around to suggest that what we are probably thinking of is more than a mythical beast. The densely woven world of kin, neighbours, friends and co-workers, highly localised and strongly caring within the confines of quite tightly defined relationships, above all the relationships of kinship. What is found in empirical research is a rough approximation to the ideal type

97

- the sort of thing that turned up again and again in the famous 'community studies' of the 1950s; in Bethnal Green, in North Wales, in St. Ebbes in the old centre of Oxford, in Yorkshire mining villages, in mid-19th century Preston and even in mid-20th century Dagenham. In all these cases localities were found permeated with informal social networks sufficiently dense, complex and extensive, and evoking sufficient commitment from residents, for a high proportion of local needs for care to be met within them (Bulmer, 1986).

He explained new (or modern) neighbourhoodism in the following way:

If mobility and choice are two distinctive features of the social effects of industralisation, formal organisation and a vastly enlarged sphere of public, political, life are two others. And it is precisely these four properties - mobility, choice, organisation and politics - that identify and precipitate modern neighbourhoodism and mark it out as something quite unlike the traditional neighbourhood. Modern neighbourhoodism is in its purest form an attempt by newcomers to create a local social world through political or quasi-political action. Great organisational skills and ingenious organisational devices are often used in attempts to mobilise old and new residents alike in order to protect amenities, enhance resources and, to a greater or lesser degree, wrench control of the local milieu from outside authorities and vest it in local hands (Bulmer, 1986).

My own view is that this second statement, with its emphasis on 'political or quasi-political action', gives a distorted picture of the new style of community. Obviously that is one element, but others include deliberately setting out to make new friends and joining local organisations (not just campaigning ones). If, however, we modify the notion of the new community to include these components as well, we have two useful contrasted models.

In practice, few if any places correspond precisely to one or the other. In the most traditional community there are usually some newcomers, lacking local kin and knowing few, if any, residents; this was true even of Bethnal Green in the 1950s. Likewise, although suburban Woodford at the same date was predominantly the new kind of community, some of its residents had lived there a long time and some had relatives nearby - and such people were by no means confined to the working classes. It is a matter of balance, some districts being predominantly traditional in style, others predominantly new, yet others a more complex blend.

Despite the earlier quotation from Philip Abrams about the 'demise' of traditional communities his study of ten areas itself showed that, in his words, they were 'not entirely a thing of the past ... we have come across two, possibly three, localities in which something plainly identifiable as an attenuated version of the traditional neighbourhood systems of relationships could be recognised' (Bulmer, 1986). It is, however, also clear that the balance has been changing. There are now more communities in which attachments have been built up in the new ways, and those communities which are still substantially traditional are less so than the past. More places, for more residents, are near the 'new' end of the spectrum rather than the 'traditional'.

A more important question, irrespective of the sources of such attachments as there are in territorial communities, is about the distribution of localities (and the people living in them) along another scale, in terms of the degree of attachment community. Some people have few contacts - or even none - with other residents, some have little - or no - sense of identity with their area, and the proportions of such people differ from district to district. In trying to assess the current position in Britain, I shall look at the two aspects - interrelationships and identity - in turn.

There is strong evidence from a range of sources that the overwhelming majority of people have reasonably 'friendly' (if often superficial) social contacts with neighbours, and that most do have some personal friends living locally. If the criterion is the experience of the majority of residents, most districts in Britain exhibit what might be described as at least a moderate degree of local interaction.

Less is known about the other element. The last national study on people's sense of identity with their area, already referred to, was the community attitudes survey in 1967, when nearly four people out of every five reported some feeling of attachment to their 'home' community area. Local surveys at around the same date or a few years later mostly had similar results, exceptions being ones in inner city areas in Lambeth in 1973 (Shankland et al., 1977) and Southwark in 1975 (Prescott-Clarke and Hedges, 1976), where only 35 per cent and 40 per cent respectively responded positively to rather different but roughly comparable questions. If the national survey were repeated now it is possible that the proportions would be lower than in 1967, and one would certainly expect variations between places, with inner areas scoring low.

But it seems unlikely that British society as a whole has changed so much since that date that the general picture would be dramatically reversed. Apart from anything else, such a result would contradict the findings on local social networks, including that from the 1982 MORI Survey on neighbours reported in Chapter IV. We know from the special analysis by Janowitz and Kasarda (1974) that the two elements - interrelationships and identity - were strongly interdependent then, and that relationship too is unlikely to have been drastically weakened. It seems that it probably remains true that for most people, and therefore most places, there is some sense of local identity.

The earlier discussion about the factors influencing local attachment points clearly to the kinds of people who usually have less to do with others and have less sense of identification with their local residential area. Such people are often newcomers, single people, young and middle-aged couples without dependent children, couples who both work outside the home, and those who for whatever reason have personal inhibitions about mixing. The kinds of places are clear too: above all districts where there are large proportions of these very sorts of people or where the physical form is discouraging, for example certain kinds of 'mass-housing' estates of flats.

Conclusion
Contrary to popular belief, in present-day Britain most localities, for most people, have something of the character of a community of attachment. At the neighbourhood scales, territorial communities are seldom just that and nothing more. But some important qualifications need to be added.

The first is that what has been reported should not conjure up a picture of a mosaic of small identifiable local communities. As has been made clear earlier, at the most local scale few areas have clearly defined boundaries about which all residents agree. The perception of a local precinct or of the wider physical neighbourhood is largely a subjective matter. Secondly, the decline of the traditional working-class community undoubtedly means that, in the course of this century at least, there has been a long-term reduction in the number and proportion of places with dense local networks and a strong sense of local solidarity. The newer styles of developing community ties work well enough for their purpose, for most people, but the outcome is more attenuated, less all-embracing than the traditional pattern. It also excludes those who, because they are too timorous or lack relevant experience, do not find it easy to establish new relationships.

The positive side is that most people now have more choice about how fully they will participate in their residential community. They can decide to have nothing to do with their neighbours or with local affairs; or they can choose to become heavily engaged in their locality. This voluntary character of local attachment has been summed up well in the term 'community of limited liability' (Janowitz, 1967). This idea contains two aspects: 'on the one hand, residents were seen as having a choice about where they could live and how much they would participate in the local community ... On the other hand, the community of limited liability emphasised ... the purposeful creation of a community which provided a common way of life to people living in close proximity' (Janowitz and Suttles, 1978).

Related to this conclusion is a final point, about the increased role of dispersed networks and dispersed communities of interest. Their rise has meant that local attachments now constitute only one pattern of social life among others, and can therefore be taken up or largely ignored (according to choice). Local ties are inevitably weaker than they have historically been, because they overlap much less often than they used to with other ties, of kinship, friendship, work, leisure and other interests. The multiplicity of strands which reinforce local social relationships have been separating out since the Industrial Revolution, the process having been accelerated by developments in transport and communications - and particularly, over the last four decades, the spread in car ownership.

In conclusion, local community undoubtedly matters in the lives of the great majority of people in Britain. But, also for the great majority, ties with relatives, friends and others now extend far beyond the local area, and the neighbourhood or local community does not encompass the social networks of most people, not even among those identified earlier as relatively tied to locality. Most residents look beyond their neighbourhood for most of their social relationships, often including those most important to them. These changes have obvious implications when looking at sources of support, which are among the concerns of the final chapter.

Table IV.1 Hierarchy of Urban Local Communities

Title	Description	Population size
Precinct (or immediate neighbourhood)	Same and adjacent streets/blocks of flats	Several hundred
Neighbourhood	Functional or identifiable larger area, up to about the size of a ward	Between about 3,000 and and 10,000
District or small town	Smaller district council area; small town	Between about 25,000 and 75,000
Larger district or town	Larger district council area (including metropolitan district council); larger town	Up to about 250,000

VII IMPLICATIONS FOR POLICY AND RESEARCH

Any attempt to draw general conclusions from this review is bound to depend on a personal interpretation of the various sets of findings. My own view is that the picture that has emerged is one not only of change but also of continuity. There are four broad themes.

First, reflecting the increase in the housing stock since 1945, there has been a decline in the proportion of people living in the same household as relatives, and at the same time an increased geographical spread of kinship networks. But rising living standards and above all improvements in communications have made it possible for contacts to remain at high levels. Relatives, particularly women relatives, continue to provide the bulk of help and support, not only in emergencies and at critical stages in life but for many also on a day-to-day, or at least week-to-week, basis. The characteristic new kinship pattern is the 'dispersed extended family', with regular meetings and support despite the absence of propinquity.

Secondly, friendship networks too have become more spread geographically, and dispersed 'interest communities' have become more dominant at the expense of local groupings. Nowadays most of the informal relationships of most people are not local.

Thirdly, these changes in social life originated, like so many others in the past (see Young and Willmott, 1973), with upper and middle-class people and at present are more common among them. But with long-term increases in mobility - both residential and from ones home - the new patterns are gradually becoming more general. Though class differences remain, and are particularly marked for instance in wealth, in income and in conditions at work, people's informal relationships are in one sense becoming more homogeneous. In another sense, of course, the wider choice that is made possible through greater mobility - and hence accessibility - creates opportunities for greater diversity.

103

Fourthly, none of this means that local ties, local affiliations and local loyalties have no place in people's lives. They remain of some importance to the great majority despite the dispersal of informal - and other - relationships. Like kinship and friendship, neighbourhood relationships have not atrophied but have instead adapted to the changed conditions in life.

It has been fashionable to deplore the decline of kinship and local community, as it was among some of the early sociologists cited in the first chapter, and to lament the supposed consequences for informal care. But, although fewer people than in the past now have relatives close at hand and few are surrounded by long-standing neighbours, kinship and, for its characteristic functions, neighbouring are alive and well, while friends are at least as available as in earlier periods.

On one argument informal relationships of these kinds are indeed of more importance than ever. They are certainly central to a transformation currently taking place in the political life of Britain and other advanced societies: a counter-movement to the increased scale and remoteness of institutions, public and private, that has been so marked since 1945. The new mood is endorsed, with different emphasis, by all the major political parties. It is expressed in such diverse but compatible notions as reducing the power of the state, recognising that 'small is beautiful', decentralising local services and encouraging a range of so-called community policies, from community medicine to community policing (Willmott, 1984). In social policy in particular, the key phrases are 'community care' and 'supporting informal carers'.

The potential contribution of informal social networks to these trends is evident enough. So is the importance of more knowledge and better understanding. The evidence presented in previous chapters is encouraging. It shows the overwhelming contribution to social care made by relatives and the general readiness of neighbours to be helpful (even if within defined limits). On the other hand, it indicates the sort of people likely to lack social networks and informal care, including elderly people without children and families with severely handicapped members.

But current knowledge is limited. As the Barclay Report (1982) put it when advocating services which would work more closely with informal carers, 'we still know too little about what determines the shape and style of informal networks'. For a start, policy-makers need to know far more precisely how many people, in different degrees of need and at different stages in life, have access to informal care. How many, for example, are living near to relatives, how many in the kinds of district where neighbours are ready to help?

Forms of care

As well as understanding more about what people themselves do, there is a need for appropriate policies to promote, sustain and substitute for informal care. In discussing the role of informal care or help, a more systematic set of distinctions is needed than that so far employed. Adapting and re-labelling the categories used by Bayley and his colleagues in their action research project in Dinnington, South Yorkshire (Seyd et al., 1984), I propose to distinguish between the following four broad types of informal care, moving from the most demanding to the least. (Although the emphasis here is on informal support, it will be obvious that virtually all of these things can be done by offical, or sometimes voluntary, services.)

Personal care. This, sometimes called intimate care, also corresponds to what Roy Parker described as 'tending'. Examples are washing, bathing, dressing, taking to the toilet, lifting and feeding a disabled or infirm person, or cleaning up an incontinent person.

Domestic care. This includes such household tasks as cooking, house-cleaning, laundering clothes and bedlinen.

Auxiliary care. This is intended to cover practical help that is less demanding than the two preceding categories. Bayley's examples are collecting prescriptions, shopping, gardening, odd household jobs and providing transport. The list can be augmented to cover home decorations and repairs, financial help and help in kind, including loans.

Social support. The Dinnington researchers describe this as covering 'visits made for social purposes'; their emphasis is on such activities as sitting, talking and exchanging news, but the category can usefully be extended to include advice, informal counselling and emotional support. Social support is the most problematic category, since visiting in itself is not usually regarded as help or care, and would not, for example, normally be applied to a visit by one young able-bodied person to another, or by a young family to their middle-aged parents or parents-in-law. But the Dinnington team are surely right to include it; as they point out, social visiting particularly for elderly and disabled people has an important function to play in maintaining their well-being and checking on their day-to-day health (Seyd et al., 1984).

Another type of help is not substantial enough to be added as a fifth category but important enough in the general scheme of informal support to deserve mention here. This is the surveillance described in Chapter IV as something that is often done by neighbours for people who are vulnerable but lack local carers; it can also be provided by postmen or milk roundsmen.

In terms of the four main types of informal care, a further distinction can usefully be made - between sustained care and other kinds. Care may be needed in an emergency, as when a young normally-fit mother with dependent children is ill enough to stay in bed, and thus needs help in caring for the children. Care may be required only occasionally or on an intermittent basis, such as taking a housebound person out for occasional trips in a car, doing repairs or maintenance as needed for those who cannot do them for themselves, buying new clothes for an elderly person. Or it may be the kind of continuing - or sustained - personal or domestic care needed by a severely disabled person or an elderly infirm person.

The Dinnington study, though it does not make such distinctions, provides a useful picture of the distribution of the four kinds of care among the local 'users' of statutory services, four-fifths of whom were elderly, mostly aged 75 or over. About one user in every eight was receiving informal personal care, half of them getting it from someone in the same household, and half from someone living elsewhere. The proportion of people receiving other forms of care was higher, and the less demanding the care was the higher the proportion who received it. In Wenger's (1984) general sample of people aged 65 and over in rural areas in North Wales, a smaller proportion than in Dinnington - one person in twenty - received personal care from informal sources and a quarter had regular help with 'routine chores', a category broadly corresponding, in the terminology of this chapter, to a mixture of domestic and auxiliary care.

With the Dinnington users of services and with the more infirm members of Wenger's sample, much of the care had to be continuing rather than occasional. That does not apply, however, to the bulk of the country's population. Of the total amount of informal help provided from outside the nuclear family, relatively little needs to be sustained. The most demanding care - sustained, and also personal or domestic - is the exception rather than the rule. This is just as well, given the strain it can put upon the informal carers and the fact that those who do not receive such care on an informal basis are precisely the people for whom institutional care is the main alternative.

Locality and care

As shown by a number of research studies, for elderly people care is often provided within the household by spouses, usually themselves elderly, or by children or children-in-law with whom, often, the parents have gone to live when they become infirm. It is usually provided at home by parents for their handicapped children, whether young or adult. But what about help from outside the household?

The Dinnington team begin with the assumption, based partly on Bayley's earlier work (1973), that the bulk of care was local; one aim of the study had been to test this. On the basis of their research they reported:

> ... in general the premise that informal care is locally based holds true, though more so for care given by friends (or neighbours) than by relatives.

As might have been expected, they also found that 'the more demanding the task the more likely it was that the carer lived in the village'; more visits for social support or auxiliary care 'were made by people living outside Dinnington'.

The social pattern of a Yorkshire village may differ from those in other types of area. More important, the members of the Dinnington sample were users of official services, and mainly very elderly, and therefore often needed sustained care. It is clear that, in addition to some support from official services, such people depend on at least one informal carer living locally, particularly if the care has to be personal or domestic. But even for such people some further contribution is often made by relatives or friends who live at a distance, as long as they are reasonably accessible - say within half an hour's car drive for domestic care during the week, and up to about two hours drive away for auxiliary help or social support.

With people at other stages in life locality is less important, although the propensity of young parents in particular to build up a network of local friends has been noted. Such local networks usually provide some help in childbirth or an occasional illness, but a common pattern is for the wife's mother, or another relative, to travel even quite a long distance to do the personal or domestic caring needed and also for parents or other kin to provide auxiliary care and social support from outside the locality.

A network of local carers - and potential carers - is a valuable resource for people at any stage in life, and personal care obviously depends on propinquity, even if only temporary propinquity when the need is intermittent. But, to sum up on this point, not all those providing care need to live locally. Dispersed networks, and in particular what in Chapter II I have called dispersed extended families and dispersed kinship networks, can and often do contribute some forms of care. Distance is not an insurmountable barrier. In this sense, it is misleading to give the impression, as is sometimes done, that all or even necessarily most care comes from within the local community. What happens in practice depends on the care needed, on the circumstances of the person needing it and on the geographical distribution of their networks, particularly of kinship.

Informal care, today and tomorrow

Perhaps the most striking finding from the body of research is that the bulk of care comes from close relatives. This is especially true of personal and domestic care, and especially so when the need for it is continuous: 'The more demanding the care the more likely it is to come from kin' (Seyd et al., 1984). But this does not mean that other relationships are negligible as sources. As shown in earlier chapters there is substitution by more genealogically distant relatives when closer ones are absent and by friends, even neighbours, when no relatives at all are available. The limits to this process need, however, to be borne in mind. Non-relatives are seldom willing to give personal care, particularly on a long-term basis, and in any event those needing the care apparently often have difficulty in accepting it from them. Nevertheless, neighbours and local friends can and do help even with personal matters in an emergency and, together with non-local friends, provide forms of auxiliary help - such as shopping, gardening, house maintenance and social support.

The greater the need (as measured by the extent of disability or ill-health) the more likely people are to respond to it by providing care (Bayley et al., 1985). But it does not follow from this that everybody who needs informal care receives it, or receives enough. As has been made clear, informal care is patchy; some kinds of people - elderly people without children, parents with severely handicapped children - are less likely than others to receive it.

This points up the issues central to policy: the capacity of informal carers to provide support and the measures needed to help them to do so. The government's aim, as noted in the introductory chapter, is to draw increasingly upon such sources of care. It is an aim that has developed under successive governments since the late 1950s, and the arguments for it have changed over time. The main emphases now are on the need to contain public spending, on the advantages of informal care as against other forms and on consumer choice. These are particularly relevant to the current policy debate about 'welfare pluralism', the starting point of which is the government's suggestion that the balance of care-provision should shift from statutory sources to private, voluntary and informal ones.

There will be difficulties in ensuring that sufficient informal carers are available in the future to meet the need. For one thing, the demographic trends are not favourable. The main need for sustained personal and domestic care comes from people aged 80 and over, whose numbers will increase steeply over the next thirty years. Meanwhile the numbers of adult children available to do the caring are falling; this is a continuation of a long-term fall in the ratio of potential carers to cared-for (Moroney, 1976).

As well as such demographic trends there are others. The research has shown time and again that the relatives who do most of the personal domestic caring are daughters and daughters-in-law, with sons and sons-in-law, along with other relatives, providing auxiliary help and sharing in social support. Apart from the fact that, because of falling family size, there will be fewer daughters and daughters-in-law in the future, the steady increase in employment among married women in recent decades suggests that more are likely to have careers or be in other paid work. The consequences of the increase in divorce and remarriage over the past fifteen years are as yet unknown. And changes in women's attitudes towards their roles may make them less willing to undertake heavy and demanding care on a long-term basis. The sense of kinship obligation which has in the past led women to take up such burdens may not necessarily continue at present levels (see Finch and Groves, 1980).

Yet there are, as Bosanquet (forthcoming) argues, some trends which may perhaps make informal caring easier than in the past. People have more spacious, more comfortable and better-equipped homes, so that they can more easily have others to stay with them for a period. The miniaturisation of machines such as freezers, washing machines and television makes life easier for carers. The steady decline in working hours, together with the increase in unemployment and early retirement, means that there is potentially more time available, particularly among men. These mitigating influences apart, the balance is, nevertheless, likely to be against rather than for an increase in the resources available for informal care.

Linking formal and informal care

The stated aim of official policy is to ensure that such potential resources for informal care as are available are used as fully and effectively as possible (see, for example, Department of Health and Social Security, 1981). If this is to became a reality on a substantial scale it is essential that the formal services collaborate with and support the informal carers. The task has sometimes been described as that of 'interweaving' care from the two sources. Although this already happens, for example when home helps complement what is done by relatives and neighbours, a number of studies suggest that the present arrangements often fall short of doing this. The Dinnington study of users noted that:

> In spite of the considerable overlap between the statutory services and informal carers ... there was little reported contact between them (Seyd et al., 1984).

A wider review of research on informal care concluded:

> The evidence we are able to glean from various sources suggests that available services are likely to have little overall effect for informal carers ... few dependent people who have informal carers appear to receive services and, when they do, such services are usually crisis-orientated rather than a part of long-term support (Parker, 1985).

There is a high degree of consensus about what, in general terms, is needed from the formal services if the desired meshing is to be achieved. The Seebohm Report (1968) said that the authorities had to recognise that the two sectors were 'complementary', Bayley (1973) that the objective was 'sensitive coordination ... a partnership' in which the contribution of informal care was 'seen, recognised and acknowledged'; the Barclay Report (1982) sought 'the development of flexible decentralised patterns of organisation based upon a social care plan which takes full account of informal care, and mobilises voluntary and statutory provision in its support'. It is recognised that this kind of response depends

110

upon effective day-to-day co-operation between the various health and local authority services themselves, and between them and local voluntary bodies, as well as between all these and the informal carers and cared-for.

All this, of course, is much more difficult than it sounds to achieve in practice. Co-ordination of services and ensuring 'flexible sensitivity' pose problems for all formal organisations. Then, as Johnson and Cooper (1983) point out in their review of research on informal care, 'many informal care arrangements are, by their very informality, extremely fragile and sensitive to outside influence'; they go on to cite two studies which showed that 'in some circumstances the intrusion of professionals into an informal care relationship or system can have highly counter-productive effects' (see Bytheway and Hall, 1979 and Mellet, 1980).

There can also be difficulties over the roles of professional workers. For one thing, those roles and the expectations that go with them are different from those of informal carers:

> Being employed to provide care establishes certain expectations, including the notion of fixed duration - hours of work or a shift - while informal care, particularly in the family, has no beginning or end unless relief is available ... It cannot be assumed that the two will happily exist side by side (Bulmer, 1986).

Wenger (1984) remarks that:

> The interface between formal and informal care and between agencies is fraught with difficulties (particularly over boundaries of responsibility and budgeting).

Pinker, in his minority report to Barclay, expressed concern about the conflict of responsibilities that might result from 'community social work', and also about the danger that, in the process of seeking out and promoting informal support, workers in formal services might intrude upon the privacy both of the potential carers and of those receiving the care.

The experiments
The difficulties are mentioned, not because they are insuperable, but because it is as well to be realistic about the magnitude of the task. Fortunately there have been, in recent years, a number of monitored experiments into alternative ways of connecting up the formal and informal sectors. Three major action projects have

been supported by the Department of Health and Social Security. The Department has, incidentally, also funded many of the relevant research studies, including those by Philip Abrams and his colleagues on neighbourhood care schemes, by Wenger on the support networks of elderly people, and by Sinclair and his colleagues on informal support for elderly clients of social services.

Two of the three action projects are in almost complete contrast to each other. One is in Normanton, Yorkshire (Hadley and McGrath, 1984). 'Patch' social work has been introduced in as many as eighty-five local authorities; the detailed arrangements vary. In Normanton the patch system included domiciliary and ancillary social services as well as social work; domiciliary and ancillary staff were recruited locally and integrated into patch teams led by social workers.

The essence of any patch scheme is that a small team is responsible for social care in its area - in Normanton it serves a population of 5,000-8,000. The workers in this team get to know the area and the population well and thus, so the argument goes, are able to work closely with informal carers and encourage informal initiatives. Because the team is local and accessible there are many informal referrals. Responsibility for social work is largely devolved to the team, and its members decide on priorities - who is to receive help and support of different kinds - in a way that is more responsive to local perceptions of need than would be possible with more conventional social work.

The second project is the Kent Community Care scheme in Thanet, a seaside area with a large population of elderly people (Challis and Davies, 1985). In this scheme priority attention is focussed upon those frail elderly people who are at risk of entering residential care. The social workers, acting as 'case managers' are given a budget of up to two-thirds of the cost of residential care for each such person, and have responsibility 'for the co-ordination and development of care for the elderly people' (Challis and Davies, 1980). The idea is to assemble all available support to the same end. The other local authority services are drawn upon, as are medical services, including specialist geriatricians. All this is co-ordinated with care provided by local people, and some payment can be made for that care.

The major new resource, developed with the budget, proved to be the use of local people as helpers, whether or not previously part of the elderly person's social network, to perform specified tasks for individuals, usually for relatively

112

small payments, interwoven with the help from more formal services such as home help and district nursing (Challis, 1985).

The contrasts with Normanton could hardly be more marked. In Normanton the priorities are set by social workers and ancillary workers in the light of their dealings with local people; in Kent they are laid down in advance to concentrate services where they will promote a range of community care precisely for those seen as in greatest need. In Normanton the social workers are generalists, working with the full range of local people and their problems; in Kent they are specialists in geriatric care, and therefore knowledgeable about the more relevant specialist services and personnel. The Normanton scheme focusses on people in the context of their neighbourhood, the Kent scheme on people in the context of potential forms of support for them, including potential informal carers. Normanton is thus a form of geographical decentralisation, for general needs, Kent of resource decentralisation for a specific one (Challis, 1985). Both, in their different ways, promote community care and in particular the interweaving of formal and informal support which is the aim of policy.

The third main DHSS-funded scheme, the Dinnington project, whose research findings on informal care have already been referred to, is another variant. The project at the Rotherham area of South Yorkshire was like Normanton in being 'community-based' but gave more emphasis to collaborative working at the local level between the various statutory services, particularly social services, housing, education, welfare and health services. The aim was to encourage all these to 'work closely with all informal carers, whether family, friends or neighbours, and also with voluntary groups and individual volunteers' (Bayley et al., 1981). One innovation was a regular fortnightly meeting of all professional workers. The project stimulated the creation of local groups geared to people's needs; through one such group volunteers provided transport, for instance, for elderly people, while another helped in the care of seriously ill people at home.

So far the full final report of only the Normanton project has been published, though a series of reports have come from Dinnington and from Kent. There were some setbacks in all three projects. For example the Normanton team and, even more, the Dinnington team explain that full implementation was impeded by practical difficulties, including problems of collaboration. Furthermore in the Dinnington project it was not found as easy as had been hoped for the statutory workers to co-operate with informal carers, and also the evidence from before and after surveys did not show that either service users or their carers were more 'satisfied' with the new system than the previous arrangements.

Nevertheless, the three teams of researchers clearly believe that they achieved marked success. Hadley and McGrath say that their evidence 'suggests that the Normanton team helped proportionately more of those at risk than the neighbourly client-oriented team (in the "comparison" area) ... and that it was much more effective in community development. Further ... the range and quality of its work appeared to be at least as good ... '. Challis (1985) reports of the Kent scheme: 'The evidence suggests that it reduced admissions to residential care and improved the quality of life of frail elderly people without imposing extra burdens on principal carers or additional costs on the statutory services'. Bayley and his colleagues (1985) conclude about Dinnington: 'We have been able to show considerable improvements in the way the service has been delivered and we think there are substantial achievements ... The balance sheet is complex but ... we judge that there were solid and substantial gains'.

The reports do show that the three experiments were useful attempts at developing collaboration with informal carers, and achieved worthwhile practical results. They may have done much more, as the researchers assert. It is not possible at this stage, without a thorough sifting of all the findings, to make a proper assessment of the three experiments, or draw out the implications including conclusions about the best methods or combination of methods to develop a partnership with informal sources of care.

Such experiments certainly suggest, however, that it is possible to achieve some success. As well as the three discussed, there have also been others. Some are further extensions of the original projects; for example, the Kent Community Care team has established similar schemes, but with variations, in Gateshead, North Wales and other parts of Kent. There have also been - and are - other examples of community-based care (see for example Harbert and Rogers, 1983; Young, 1985) and many local warden schemes and Good Neighbour projects, including one in Wales (Bytheway and Hall, 1979) and those studied by Philip Abrams and his colleagues (Abrams et al., 1981; Bulmer, 1986). Though these projects vary widely in the rigour of their evaluation, some producing little more than descriptive reports of innovative schemes, they are useful in contributing to the body of knowledge about developments in community care. When brought together and thoroughly assessed, they could provide useful pointers for policy.

Meanwhile, some general principles are already clear.

Recognition of informal care. In one sense the contribution of informal carers is officially recognised, certainly at national level: the policy is based on such a recognition. But there has to be an explicit acknowledgment of its importance at all levels, together with an explicit policy of working with them, supporting them and promoting their participation. Without such a comprehensive recognition there is unlikely to be enough drive to achieve successful care by the community.

Decentralisation. There needs to be some decentralisation of functions and of responsibilities, whether to a small-scale local area, as in Normanton and Dinnington, or to the networks and potential networks of clients as in the Kent scheme (where budgets were also decentralised). Without focussing down in some way, and giving a large degree of autonomy to the professional workers most directly responsible, it is likely to be difficult to work with informal carers in a flexible and responsive way.

Inter-service collaboration. Since one of the biggest obstacles is the difficulty of co-ordination between the different services, some form of joint working is essential, embracing the various departments of the local authority (including social workers, home helps, local wardens if they exist, housing welfare workers, education welfare workers) and the medical services (including district nurses, general practitioners, community psychiatric workers). Workers in residential services, providing short-term and long-term care, also need to be involved. One useful arrangement is a regular meeting of local professional workers, like the fortnightly meetings held in Dinnington and elsewhere.

Co-terminosity of boundaries. The various services (including departments of the same authority) apparently continue to operate for the most part on the basis of different local boundaries, and this in itself hinders collaboration and makes things difficult for clients and carers alike. Co-terminosity should be the aim. If some differences have to remain the services should at least work out means of co-operating flexibly across their boundaries.

115

Support for Good Neighbour, self-help and voluntary groups.
Voluntary Good Neighbour schemes, as the research shows,
can provide useful support and can be useful bridges between
local people and formal services. The same applies to self-
help groups of the types mentioned in Chapter V, and to local
voluntary groups of various kinds, including church groups.
As a matter of policy, local authorities and medical services
should, as many already do, support these initiatives and seek
to collaborate with them.

Training. These new perspectives need to be reflected in
training, so that professional workers and service managers
are fully aware of the existence and contribution of informal
care, and likewise of the objectives, the difficulties and the
best ways to work effectively with the informal and
voluntary sectors.

Learning from innovation. There neither is nor ever will be
one perfect arrangement to sustain informal care or to
provide a substitute for it (as Good Neighbour schemes do),
and in this sense the more experiments there are the better.
In any event public authorities will continue to develop their
own local innovations in community care. It is, however,
important that such new initiatives should be carefully
monitored and, where possible, designed as experiments with
'control' populations not exposed to new schemes. It is also
necessary to build up directories of local experiments and
innovations. Some such directories already exist (for example
Cloke, 1983; Ferlie et al., 1984; Social Work Service
Development Group, 1984; Tinker, 1984), but there would be
value in pushing the idea further.

In addition to these general points there is enough material
from a range of studies of informal care to offer specific
suggestions about how best to support them, most of these
measures being among the hoped-for results of linking the formal
and informal sectors. The issues are discussed in reports for
example by Allen (1983a, 1983b), Levin et al., (1983), Wenger
(1984), Parker (1985) and Bulmer (1986). Obviously, the support
needed varies according to the condition and needs of the person
being cared for, whether a severely handicapped child, an infirm
elderly person or a mentally confused person. Most of the
following suggestions are already implemented to some extent and
in some areas, but they can usefully be extended.

Early identification. The official services need to be alerted early to the need to help carers, for example through the general practitioner, rather than when the supporters are already exhausted. At the same time care must be taken to avoid what seems like an intrusion at a stage before the problems have become acute.

Counselling and moral support. Carers providing sustained domestic and, even more, personal care particularly benefit from recognition of their task by professional services, and from the opportunity to discuss their problems with a sympathetic listener. Counselling and moral support, along with practical, can create what Allen (1983b) calls a 'care partnership' between informal carer and professional. The initial offer of such support poses delicate problems for professionals, however, since they will want to avoid the possible intrusion just mentioned.

Information. There need to be effective local information services and schemes so that carers can readily discover where to go for support and what help is available for them (Equal Opportunities Commission, 1982).

Fiscal policy. Support for carers requires that the government adapts the fiscal system to this end (Equal Opportunities Commission, 1982; Finch and Groves, 1983). As Bulmer puts it: 'the tax and social security position of informal carers is in many ways disadvantageous. Married women who give up work are particularly penalised, both in terms of the tax burden on the family and in not being entitled to Invalid Care Allowance. Additionally, their pensions suffer'. There would obviously be costs in making the kinds of changes implied but, because the support for carers should increase informal care and thus reduce the burden on public services, the net financial effect should be slight.

Regular breaks for carers. These can be provided through short-stay residential care, though the form of this care is important (Allen, 1983b), and also by fostering services and by giving domiciliary support which allows carers to take holidays.

<u>Regular help with personal and domestic care.</u> Apart from the home help service, examples are visits by district nurses for nursing care, domiciliary relief care at night as well as during the day, and incontinence laundry services. There are of course inescapable costs in providing resources to make such domiciliary services adequate enough to meet all needs.

As well as supporting the carers, some measures can provide substitute care in the community for those who lack informal networks. Good Neighbour schemes are intended to do just that; volunteers - or sometimes local people who are paid a small fee - give some of the care and support usually given by relatives, friends or existing neighbours. The paid helpers recruited into the Kent Community Care project provide another example, and street warden schemes yet another. Many self-help groups provide similar scope for substitute care.

As was noted in the introductory chapter, the boundary between informal care and this kind of care is a fluid one. The relationship between a paid or voluntary carer and the person cared for often develops into personal friendship, in the same way as sometimes happens between the fellow-members of a self-help group. At the same time, it seems that schemes to create substitutes for informal carers are more likely to succeed if some payment is made; this was one of the conclusions from the Good Neighbour research by Philip Abrams, and was suggested by a study by Diana Leat (1982) of family placement schemes for elderly people. It is certainly what is done in Kent. Whatever the detailed arrangements, it is clear that, as has been implied earlier, the range of policies needs to include forms of substitute care for those who lack the informal carers.

Informal care is influenced by broader policies than those directly concerned with the organisation of services. Another example is in housing and planning. Since personal relationships largely determine the chances of receiving informal care when needed, it is sensible to examine policies that might affect people's proximity to relatives and other potential carers, or might have a bearing on people's attachment to neighbours, as discussed in the previous chapter.

In the 1950s Michael Young and I (1957) argued that post-war planning and housing policies were tending to break settled residence in inner areas, and thus disperse existing networks of kinship and neighbourhood, even when people wanted to stay together, and that this in turn was bound to affect the availability of informal support. The study by Coates and Silburn in

Nottingham, cited in Chapter II, suggested, on the other hand, that under certain conditions public housing could make it easy for kin to live nearer each other if they wished.

Housing policies have changed since the period in which we wrote - and since 1976 when Coates and Silburn did their research. In particular, it seems likely that the sale of council houses, in reducing the stock of homes for rent, also limits the opportunities of relatives to choose to live near each other. There is, therefore, a case for a review of the impact on social networks of recent housing policies. It certainly remains important, meanwhile, for central and local authorities, in determining policies and plans, to consider their implications for informal support.

Priorities for research
The final part of this chapter looks more closely at research, offering not a large programme for immediate implementation but some ideas for consideration in determining research priorities over the next few years.

The lack of up-to-date information on informal relationships has been evident throughout. Most of the community studies cited were done a quarter of a century ago. From the mid-1960s there was a reaction against such local studies on the part of most researchers, reflecting a more 'structural' approach to understanding society and its problems; community studies were rejected on the grounds that they distracted attention from national economic, political and social structures, which were rightly seen as important determinants of people's opportunities and welfare.

The inherent limitation of community studies is that each can speak with authority about only one small geographical area, whose patterns cannot be extrapolated to a broader population. Their compensating advantage - which justifies their having some place in the battery of research tools - is that they can show, as no other method can, something of the interrelationship between different elements of local life, in particular between people's daily lives on the one hand and the local institutions of society on the other.

There has been a recent small revival of interest in local studies, examples being Pahl, 1984 and Wallman, 1984, but these do not contribute much to the subject-matter of this review. There would, therefore, be a case for a further round of local studies in contrasted areas - in, for example, inner city districts, in suburbs, in small and medium-sized towns. Such studies would have to acknowledge, as the earlier generation of enquiries sometimes failed to do, the influence of external institutions and networks; in

119

particular, they would need to devote as much attention to informal social relationships which link residents to other people outside the locality - their dispersed networks - as to those inside it. Such studies should also devote special attention to the role of the self-conscious, often quasi-political, groupings which have flourished in the last fifteen years or so under neighbourhood and community banners, and which include some manifestations of the 'new neighbourhoodism' as described by Philip Abrams.

Even a clutch of such local studies, however, could not provide a national picture, showing for example the distribution nationally, regionally and by urban density and urban form of the various kinship types suggested in Chapter II or of neighbourhoods measured by the indices of interaction and identity used in Chapter VI. In terms of policy there is a particularly strong case for a national sample survey of people's informal relationships with others. The supply of informal care is just as much a national resource as Britain's coal or oil stocks, and it therefore needs to be properly assessed, perhaps on a regular basis, say every five years. Some relevant information has been, and more will be, collected through the official General Household Survey, but this will still fall far short of what would be needed for a proper review. The findings of any relevant surveys would need to be related to data on demographic trends and projections, which would help in looking ahead to see how the 'stock' of informal care was changing and likely to change.

There are no technical difficulties about the most basic questions to be asked in such a survey, for example on the residence of and frequency of contact with parents, children and other relatives, contacts with and help from neighbours and people's sense of identity with their locality. Asking about friends poses more of a problem, for the reasons explained in Chapter III. Further work is needed to clarify what people mean by the language of friendship and to devise appropriate methods of research on friends and friendship networks. A current small study by the author of friendship among families with children in a London suburb will make a contribution here, but is no more than a beginning.

There are other specific gaps. One is about the effect of divorce and separation on people's social networks. Chapter V cited some relevant (if outdated) evidence, the main conclusion being that social relationships were, as might have been expected, altered following divorce or separation. Friends change and kinship contacts are apparently reduced, although it is reasonable to assume that, after remarriage, kinship patterns become more complex and in some respects fuller, with new networks of parents-in-law, grandparents-in-law and others. There are particular implications for the care of elderly parents by daughters-in-law. The long-term consequences of such changes are clearly important, for informal care amongst other things. The last substantial study, done as part of a wider survey of one-parent families, was in 1970 (Hunt, 1973). In a period when divorce rates have been increasing further research is now needed. It should include not only statistical surveys such as Hunt's but also studies of a more intensive kind to throw fuller light on the changes in network patterns and their implications for informal support.

Another gap concerns social relationships at work. There are two aspects to this subject. One is that, as noted in Chapter V, there is virtually no basic knowledge about relationships with work colleagues, their meaning to people or their contribution by way of help and support. The subject is one to which industrial sociologists might be encouraged to turn their attention.

The second aspect is related to unemployment. If, as seems likely, work relationships and a sense of identity with the workplace are of some significance in the lives of those who have jobs, then the loss of this would seem to constitute another - largely unrecognised - 'dispossession' from which unemployed people suffer, along with the more obvious loss of their livelihood. White's research (forthcoming) suggests that they compensate for this deprivation, at least to some extent, by making new friends, who are presumably often unemployed as they are. But further studies of the unemployed themselves, comparing their experience with that of matched samples still in jobs, would help to illuminate the matter, indicate how far the loss of a job is indeed a 'social' deprivation, and perhaps offer suggestions for policy.

Yet another subject for research is local boundaries. Their relevance has already been made clear. If the policy aim is to develop the necessary 'interweaving' of formal and informal care, it is essential to know more about such boundaries. A number of local studies would be needed to determine the extent of co-terminosity in the various boundaries used by official services, and the relationship of those to the boundaries perceived by residents. These studies could go on to suggest ways in which the obstacles to co-terminosity could be overcome (see Shankland et al., 1977 for a discussion of the issues in the context of the Lambeth Inner Area Study).

Conclusion

This review has confirmed, if confirmation were needed, the vital importance of informal relationships. The type, range and proximity of social networks crucially affect a person's quality of life. In particular, the type: the patterns of interaction, the unwritten (and largely unarticulated) rules of conduct and above all the forms of support available vary according to the origin of social ties, whether kinship, residential propinquity or the complex and puzzling mix of opportunity, mutual attraction and social exchange we call friendship. Where possible, an attempt has been made to suggest reasons for these variations, as well as for the observed differences according to such influences as social class, stage in life and gender. Along with personal relationships, attention has also been given to collective structures, both local and dispersed, and to how and why these vary in different kinds of place and for different kinds of people.

Both in describing what happens and in debating its implications for policy and practice, current discussion depends to a disturbing degree upon conjecture rather than the facts. The gaps in knowledge are manifest, as is the case for more research and study. The best possible guidance is needed because the present official policies - which are largely non-partisan, except for differences in the emphasis to be given respectively to the statutory services on the one hand and the private commercial sector on the other - are certain to continue. The objectives of policy-makers, anyway, broadly reflect public preferences. Although there has been an expansion in private residential care for elderly people in particular, neither that nor a local authority residential home is what the majority prefer. As Wenger (1984) reported from her survey, 'Most of those interviewed expressed the desire to remain in their homes as long as they possibly could.' The policy of supporting informal care is generally endorsed, furthermore, even by most of those who give it as well as those receiving it.

There are, of course, serious anxieties about the official policy as it operates at present, particularly over the dangers of sending mentally-ill and mentally-handicapped patients out 'into the community' too precipitately (see for instance the report of the House of Commons Social Services Committee on Community Care, 1985). There is understandable scepticism about an arrangement under which citizens, especially women citizens, are expected to take on extra burdens without (as it often seems) a matching willingness to give them the recognition and backing they need. But if informal care in general can be adequately supported and meshed with formal, it will surely be a sensible and, from the point of view of those cared-for, a better way to meet their needs and enhance their freedom of choice. As societies have become more complex, a rift has widened between the real world of human fellowship and the more abstracted world of social institutions. To bridge that gap successfully would be a signal achievement. It is an endeavour to which social research can make a worthwhile contribution.

REFERENCES

Abrams, M. (1978) Beyond Three Score and Ten: a First Report on a Survey of the Elderly, Mitcham, Age Concern.

Abrams, P. (1978) 'Community care: some research problems and priorities', in J. Barnes, and N. Connelly (eds) Social Care Research, London, Bedford Square Press for Policy Studies Institute.

Abrams, P. (1980) 'Social change, social networks and neighbourhood care', Social Work Service, 22.

Abrams, P., Abrams, S., Humphrey, R. and Snaith, R. (1981) Patterns of Neighbourhood Care, Unpublished report to Department of Health and Social Security.

Allan, G.A. (1979) A Sociology of Friendship and Kinship, London, George Allen and Unwin.

Allen I. (1983a) 'The elderly and their informal carers' in Department of Health and Social Security, Services for Elderly People Living in the Community, London, HMSO.

Allen, I. (1983b) Short-Stay Residential Care for the Elderly, Report No. 616, London, Policy Studies Institute.

Baker, J. and Young, M. (eds) (1971) The Hornsey Plan: a Role for Neighbourhood Councils in the New Local Government, Third Edition, London, Association for Neighbourhood Councils.

Ball, C. and Ball, M. (1982) What the Neighbours Say: a Report on a Study of Neighbours, Berkhamstead, The Volunteer Centre.

Ballard, R. (1982) 'South Asian families', in R.M. Rapoport, M.P. Fogarty and R. Rapoport, Families in Britain, London, Routledge and Kegan Paul.

Banks, M., Ullah, P. and Warr, P. (1984) 'Unemployment and less qualified urban young people', Employment Gazette, 92(8).

Barclay Report (1982) Social Workers: Their Role and Tasks, London, Bedford Square Press for National Institute for Social Work.

Barker, J. (1984) Black and Asian Old People in Britain, Mitcham, Age Concern England.

Barnes, J.A. (1954) 'Class and committees in a Norwegian island parish', Human Relations 7(1).

Barton, A.H. (1969) Communities in Disaster, Garden City, New York, Doubleday.

Bayley, M. (1973) Mental Handicap and Community Care, London, Routledge and Kegan Paul.

Bayley, M., Parker, P., Seyd, R. and Tennant, A. (1981) Origins, Strategy and Proposed Evaluation, Neighbourhood Services Project, Dinnington, Paper No.1, Sheffield, University of Sheffield Department of Sociological Studies.

Bayley, M., Seyd, R. and Tennant, A. (1985) The Final Report, Neighbourhood Services Project, Dinnington, Paper No.12, Sheffield, University of Sheffield Department of Sociological Studies.

Bell, C. (1968) Middle Class Families, London, Routledge and Kegan Paul.

Bell, C. (1971) 'Occupational career, family cycle and extended family relations', Human Relations, 24(6).

Berger, P. (1977) Facing up to Modernity, New York, Basic Book.

Berry, F., Lee, M. and Griffiths, S. (1981) Report on a Survey of West Indian Pensioners in Nottingham, Nottingham, Nottinghamshire Social Services Department.

Berthoud, R. and Jowell, R. (1973) Creating a Community, London, Social and Community Planning Research.

Beynon, H. (1973) Working for Ford, London, Allan Lane.

Bhalla, A. and Blakemore, K. (1981) Elders of the Ethnic Minority Groups, Birmingham, All Faiths for One Race.

Blau, P.M. (1964) Exchange and Power in Social Life, New York, John Wiley.

Boissevain, J. (1974) Friends of Friends, London, Basil Blackwell.

Bosanquet, N. (forthcoming) 'Alternative solutions: service credits', in L.E.J. Chant et al., Health and Personal Social Services: Collaboration in Community Care, London, Policy Studies Institute.

Bott, E. (1957) Family and Social Network, London, Tavistock.

Bowling, A. and Cartwright, A. (1982) Life After a Death, London, Tavistock.

Brown, R.K., Brannen, P., Cousins, J.M. and Samthier, M. (1973) 'The "occupational culture" of shipbulding workers', in M.A. Smith et al., (eds) Leisure and Society in Britain, London, Allan Lane.

Bulmer, M. (1986) Neighbours: the Work of Philip Abrams, Cambridge, Cambridge University Press.
Burton, L. (1975) The Family Life of Sick Children, London, Routledge and Kegan Paul.
Butcher, H. and Crosbie, D. (1977) Pensioned Off: a Study of the Needs of Elderly People in Cleator Moor, Papers in Community Studies, No 15, York, Department of Social Administration and Social Work, University of York.
Bytheway, W. and Hall, D. (1979) Good Neighbour Project, Report of an exploratory study on good neighbours prepared for the Department of Health and Social Security, Swansea, University College.

Cartwright, A., Hockey, L. and Anderson, J.L. (1973) Life Before Death, London, Routledge and Kegan Paul.
Challis, D. (1985) 'The community care scheme: an alternative approach to decentralisation', in S. Hatch (ed) Decentralisation and Care in the Community, Discussion Paper No.10, London, Policy Studies Institute.
Challis, D. and Davies, B. (1980) 'A new approach to community care for the elderly', British Journal of Social Work, 10(1).
Challis, D. and Davies, B. (1985) 'Long-term care for the elderly: the Community Care Scheme', British Journal of Social Work, 15(6).
Charlesworth, A., Wilkin, D. and Durie, A. (1984) Carers and Services: a Comparison of Men and Women Caring for Dependent Elderly People, Manchester, Equal Opportunities Commission.
Clarke, M. (1982) 'Where is the community which cares?', British Journal of Social Work, 12(5).
Cloke, C. (1983) Caring for the Carers: A Directory of Initiatives, Mitcham, Age Concern.
Coates, K. and Silburn, R. (1980) Beyond the Bulldozer, Nottingham, University of Nottingham, Department of Adult Education.
Coleman, A. (1985) Utopia on Trial, London, Hilary Shipman.
Cunnison, S. (1966) Wages and Work Allocation, London, Tavistock.

Daniel, W.W. (1980) Maternity Rights: the Experience of Women, Report No. 588, London, Policy Studies Institute.
Dennis, N., Henriques, F. and Slaughter, C. (1956) Coal is Our Life, London, Eyre and Spottiswoode.
Department of Health and Social Security (1977) The Way Forward, London, HMSO.

Department of Health and Social Security (1981) <u>Growing Older</u>, Cmnd 8173, London, HMSO.

Driver, G. (1982) 'West Indian families: an anthropological perspective', in R.M. Rapoport, M.P. Fogarty and R. Rapoport, <u>Families in Britain</u>, London, Routledge and Kegan Paul.

Dubin, R. (1956) 'Industrial workers' world: a study of the central life interest in industrial workers', <u>Social Problems</u>, 3(3).

Durkheim, E. 1893 (1933) <u>The Division of Labour in Society</u>, translated by G. Simpson, New York, Free Press.

Economist Intelligence Unit (1982) <u>Coping With Unemployment: the Effects on the Unemployed Themselves</u>, London, Economist Intelligence Unit.

Equal Opportunities Commission (1982) <u>Who Cares for the Carers?</u>, Manchester, Equal Opportunities Commission.

Ermisch, J. and Overton, E. (1984) <u>Minimal Household Unit: a New Perspective in a Demographic and Economic Analysis of Household Formation</u>, Research Paper 84/1, London, Policy Studies Institute.

Ferlie, E., Challis, D. and Davies, B. (1984) <u>Guide to Efficiency Improving Innovations</u>, Canterbury, Personal Social Services Research Unit.

Finch, J. and Groves, D. (1980) 'Community care and the family: a case study for equal opportunities', <u>Journal of Social Policy</u>, 9(4).

Finch, J. and Groves, D. (1983) (eds) <u>A Labour of Love</u>, London, Routledge and Kegan Paul.

Firth, R., Hubert, J. and Forge, A. (1969) <u>Families and their Relatives</u>, London, Routledge and Kegan Paul.

Fischer, C.S. <u>et al.</u> (1977) <u>Networks and Places</u>, New York, Free Press.

Fischer, C.S. (1982) <u>To Dwell Among Friends</u>, Chicago, University of Chicago Press.

Frankenberg, R. (1957) <u>Village on the Border</u>, London, Cohen and West.

Frankenberg, R. (1966) <u>Communities in Britain</u>, Harmondsworth, Penguin.

Gilroy, D. (1982) 'Informal care: reality behind the rhetoric', <u>Social Work Service</u>, 30.

Glendinning, C. (1983) <u>Unshared Care: Parents and their Disabled Children</u>, London, Routledge and Kegan Paul.

Goldthorpe, J.H. (1980) Social Mobility and Class Structure in Modern Britain, Oxford, Clarendon Press.

Goldthorpe, J.H., Lockwood, D., Bechhofer, F. and Platt, J. (1969) The Affluent Worker in the Class Structure, London, Cambridge University Press.

Gorer, G. (1955) Exploring English Character, London, Cresset Press.

Gorer, G. (1971) Sex and Marriage in England Today, London, Nelson.

Graham, H. (1979) The First Months of Motherhood, York, University of York (duplicated).

Hadley, R. and McGrath, M. (1984) When Social Services are Local: the Normanton Experience, London, George Allen and Unwin.

Hallman, H.W. (1984) Neighbourhoods: Their Place in Urban Life, Sage Library of Social Research, No. 154, London, Sage.

Hampton, W. (1970) Democracy and Community, Oxford, Oxford University Press.

Harbert, W. and Rogers, P. (1983) Community-based Social Care: The Avon Experience, London, National Council of Voluntary Organisations.

Harrison, P. (1983) Inside the Inner City, Harmondsworth, Penguin.

Hill, S. (1976) The Dockers: Class and Tradition in London, London, Heinemann.

Hole, V. (1959) 'Social effects of planned rehousing', Town Planning Review, 30(2).

Holmans, A. (1981) 'Housing careers of recently married couples', Population Trends, 24.

Homans, G. (1961) Social Behaviour: Its Elementary Forms, London, Routledge and Kegan Paul.

House of Commons Social Services Committee (1985) Community Care with Special Reference to Adult Mentally Ill and Mentally Handicapped People, Vol. I, London, HMSO.

Hughes, G.A. and McGormick, B. (1985) 'Migration intentions in the UK. Which households want to migrate and which succeed?', Economic Journal, 95, Supplement.

Hunt, A. (1973) Families and Their Needs: with particular reference to one parent families, Two volumes, SS 446, London, HMSO.

Hunt, A (1978) The Elderly at Home: A Survey Carried out on Behalf of the Department of Health and Social Security, London, HMSO.

Jackson, R.M. (1977) 'Social structure and process in friendship choice' in C.S. Fischer et al., Networks and Places: Social

Relations in the Urban Setting, New York, Free Press.
Janowitz, M. (1967) The Community Press in an Urban Setting, Second Edition, Chicago, University of Chicago Press.
Janowitz, M. and Kasarda, J.D. (1974) 'The social construction of local communities', in T. Leggatt (ed) Sociological Theory and Survey Research, London, Sage.
Janowitz, M. and Suttles, G.D. (1978) 'The social ecology of citizenship', in R.C. Sarri and Y. Hasenfield (eds) The Management of Human Services, New York, Columbia University Press.
Jennings, H. (1962) Societies in the Making, London, Routledge and Kegan Paul.
Johnson, M.L. and Cooper, S. (1983) Informal Care and the Personal Social Services: an Interpretive Literature Review, London, Policy Studies Institute (duplicated).
Johnson, M. and MacDonald, C. (1983) The Caring Capacity of the Community: the Informal Network, Final report to Social Science Research Council, Newcastle-on-Tyne, University of Newcastle-on-Tyne Department of Social Policy.

Keller, S. (1968) The Urban Neighbourhood: A Sociological Perspective, New York, Random House.
Kerr, M. (1958) The People of Ship Street, London, Routledge and Kegan Paul.
Klein, J. (1965) Samples from English Cultures, Two vols., London, Routledge and Kegan Paul.
Knight, B. and Hayes, R. (1981) Self-Help in the Inner City, London, London Voluntary Service Council.
Kuper, L. (1953) 'Blueprint for living together', in L. Kuper (ed) Living in Towns, London, Cresset Press.

Leat, D. (1982) A Home from Home. A Report of a Study of Short-Term Family Placement Schemes for the Elderly, Mitcham, Age Concern.
Leat, D. (1983) Getting to Know the Neighbours: a Pilot Study of the Elderly and Neighbourly Helping, London, Policy Studies Institute.
Lee, T. (1968) 'Urban neighbourhood as a socio-spatial schema', Human Relations, 21(2).
Levin, E., Sinclair, I. and Gorbach, P. (1983) The Supporters of Confused Elderly People: Extract from the Main Report, London, National Institute for Social Work Research Unit.
Lipsey, D. (1982) 'Neighbours: what we think of the folk next door', Sunday Times, 12 December.

Litwak, E. and Szelenyi, I. (1969) 'Primary group structures and their functions: kin, neighbours and friends', American Sociological Review, 34(4).

Llewelyn-Davies, Weeks, Forestier-Walker and Bor (1977) Circumstances of Families: People and Their Relationships, London, Department of the Environment.

Lockwood, D. (1966) 'Sources of variation in working-class images of society', Sociological Review, 14/2, reprinted in M.Bulmer (ed) (1975) Working-class Images of Society, London, Routledge and Kegan Paul.

Lupton, T. (1963) On the Shop Floor: Two Studies of Workshop Organisations and Output, Oxford, Pergamon.

Market Opinion and Research International (MORI) (1982) Neighbours: Computer Tables, London, MORI (duplicated).

Marris, P. (1982) 'Attachment and society', in C.M. Parkes and J.Stevenson-Hinde (eds) The Place of Attachment in Human Behaviour, London, Tavistock.

Mellet, J. (1980) 'Self-help, mental help and the professionals', in S. Hatch (ed) Mutual Aid and Social and Health Care, Wivenhoe, ARVAC.

Mental Health Foundation (1985) The Someone to Talk to Directory, London, Routledge and Kegan Paul.

Ministry of Housing and Local Government (1970) Moving Out of a Slum, Design Bulletin 20, London, HMSO.

Mitchell, G.D., Lupton, T., Hodges, M.W. and Smith, C.S. (1954) Neighbourhood and Community, Liverpool, University Press of Liverpool.

Mitchell, J.C. (ed) (1969) Social Networks in Urban Situations, Manchester, Manchester University Press.

Mitton, R., Willmott, P. and Willmott, P. (1983) Unemployment, Poverty and Social Policy in Europe, London, Bedford Square Press.

Mogey, J.M. (1956) Family and Neighbourhood, Oxford, Oxford University Press.

Moroney, R.M. (1976) The Family and the State, London, Longman.

Morris, P. (1965) Prisoners and Their Families, London, George Allen and Unwin.

Morton-Williams, J. and Stowell, R. (1975) Smallheath, Birmingham: a Social Survey, London, Department of the Environment.

Moss, P., Bolland, G. and Foxman, R. (1983) Transition to Parenthood Project, Report to Department of Health and Social Security.

Moss, P., Plewis, I. and Bax, M. (1978) Pre-school Project, Report to Department of Health and Social Security.

National Opinion Polls (1982) 'Church-going', Political Social Economic Review, 35, London, NOP Market Research Ltd.
Newman, O. (1973) Defensible Space, London, Architectural Press.
Nisbert, R.D. (1967) The Sociological Tradition, London, Heinemann Educational Books.

Office of Population Censuses and Surveys (1981) General Household Survey 1979, London, HMSO.
Office of Population Censuses and Surveys (1982) General Household Survey 1980, London, HMSO.

Pahl, R.E. (1984) Divisions of Labour, Oxford, Blackwell.
Parker, G. (1985) With Due Care and Attention: A Review of Research on Informal Care, London, Family Policy Studies Centre.
Parker, R. (1981) in E.M. Goldberg and S. Hatch, A New Look at the Personal Social Services, Discussion Paper No.4, London, Policy Studies Institue.
Pollert, A. (1981) Girls, Wives, Factory Lives, London, Macmillan.
Prescott-Clarke, P. and Hedges, B. (1976) Living in Southwark, London, Social and Community Planning Research.

Reid, I. (1977) (revised edition 1981) Social Class Differences in Britain: a Source Book, London, Open Books.
Richardson, A. and Goodman, M. (1983) Self-Help and Social Care, Research Report No.612, London, Policy Studies Institute.
Rosser, C. and Harris, C. (1965) The Family and Social Change, London, Routledge and Kegan Paul.
Rossiter, C. and Wicks, M. (1982) Crisis or Challenge: Family Care, Elderly People and Social Policy, London, Study Commission on the Family.
Royal Commission on Local Government in England (1969) 'Representation and community: an appraisal of three surveys'. Appendix 7, Research Appendices, Vol. III, Cmnd 4040-II, London, HMSO.

Sarkissian, W. and Heine, W. (1978) Social Mix: the Bournville Experience, Bournville and Adelaide, Bournville Village Trust and South Australian Housing Trust.
Seebohm Report (1968) Report of the Committee on Local Authority and Allied Personal Social Services, Cmnd 3703, London, HMSO.

Seyd, R., Simons, K., Tennant, A. and Bayley, M. (1984) Community Care in Dinnington: Informal Support Prior to the Project, Neighbourhood Services Project, Dinnington, Paper No.3, Sheffield, University of Sheffield, Department of Sociological Studies.

Shanas, E. et al. (1968) Old People in Three Industrial Societies, London, Routledge and Kegan Paul.

Shankland, G., Willmott, P. and Jordan, D. (1977) Inner London: Policies for Dispersal and Balance, Final report of the Lambeth Inner Area Study, London, HMSO.

Shaw, L.A. (1954) 'Impressions of family life in a London suburb', Sociological Review, 2(2).

Sheldon, J.H. (1948) The Social Medicine of Old Age, London, Oxford University Press.

Simmel, G. 1905 (1969) 'The metropolis and mental life' in R. Sennett (ed) Classic Essays on the Culture of Cities, New York, Appleton-Century-Crofts.

Sinclair, I., Crosbie, D., O'Connor, P., Stanforth, L. and Vickery, A. (1984) Networks Project: a Study of Informal Care, Services and Social Work for Elderly Clients Living Alone, London, National Institute of Social Work Research Unit.

Social Work Service Development Group (1984) Supporting the Informal Carers: Fifty Styles of Caring, Department of Health and Social Security.

Sofer, C. (1970) Men in Mid-Career: a Study of British Managers and Technical Specialists, Cambridge, Cambridge University Press.

Stacey, M. (1969) Tradition and Change, London, Oxford University Press.

Stacey, M., Batstone, E., Bell, C, and Murcott, A. (1975) Power, Persistence and Change, London, Routlegde and Kegan Paul.

Tinker, A. (1981) The Elderly in Modern Society, London, Longman.

Tinker, A. (1984) Staying at Home: Helping Elderly People, London, HMSO.

Tönnies, F. 1887 (1955) Community and Association, translated by C.P. Loomis.

Townsend, P. (1957) The Family Life of Old People, London, Routledge and Kegan Paul

Townsend, P. (1968) Chapter 6, 'The structure of the family', in E. Shanas et al., Old People in Three Industrial Societies, London, Routledge and Kegan Paul.

Walker, A. (1986) 'Community care: fact and fiction' in A. Walker, P. Ekblom and N. Deakin, The Debate About Community:

Papers From a Seminar on 'Community and Social Policy', Discussion Paper No. 13, London, Policy Studies Institute.

Wallman, S. (1984) Eight London Households, London, Tavistock.

Webber, M.M. (1964) 'Order and diversity: community without propinquity', in Lowdon Wingo Jnr (ed) Cities and Space, Baltimore, John Hopkins.

Weber, M. 1922 (1961) 'Types of social organisation' in T. Parsons, E. Shils, K.D. Naegele and J.R. Pitts (eds), Theories of Society, Vol. 1, Glencoe Free Press.

Wenger, G.C. (1984) The Supportive Network: Coping with Old Age, National Institute Social Services Library, No.6, London, George Allen and Unwin.

Westwood, S. (1984) All Day, Every Day: Factory and Family in the Making of Women's Lives, London, Pluto Press.

White, M. (forthcoming) Life in Long-Term Unemployment, London, Policy Studies Institute.

Whyte, W.H. (1957) The Organisation Man, London, Cape.

Wilkin, D. (1979) Caring for the Mentally Handicapped Child, London, Croom Helm.

Williams, W.M. (1956) The Sociology of an English Village: Gosforth, London, Routledge and Kegan Paul.

Willmott, P. (1962) 'Housing density and town design in a new town', Town Planning Review, 33(2).

Willmott, P. (1963) The Evolution of a Community: a Study of Dagenham After Forty Years, London, Routledge and Kegan Paul.

Willmott, P. (1967) 'Social research in new communities', Journal of the American Institute of Planners, 33(5).

Willmott, P. and Cooney, E. W. (1963) 'Community planning and sociological research', Journal of the American Institute of Planners, 29(2).

Willmott, P. with Thomas, D. (1984) Community in Social Policy, Discussion Paper No.9, London, Policy Studies Institute.

Willmott, P. and Young, M. (1960) Family and Class in a London Suburb, London, Routledge and Kegan Paul.

Wirth, L. (1938) 'Urbanism as a way of life', American Journal of Sociology, 44 (July).

Wolfenden Report (1978) The Future of Voluntary Organisations: the Report of the Wolfenden Committee, London, Croom Helm.

Young, K. (1985) 'The East Sussex approach', in S. Hatch (ed) Decentralisation and Care in the Community, Discussion Paper No. 10, London, Policy Studies Institute.

Young, M. and Willmott, P. (1957) Family and Kinship in East London, London, Routledge and Kegan Paul.

Young, M. and Willmott, P. (1973) The Symmetrical Family, London, Routledge and Kegan Paul.

 Policy Studies Institute

The **Policy Studies Institute** is Britain's largest independent research organisation undertaking studies of economic, industrial and social policy and the workings of political institutions.

The Institute is an educational charity, not run for profit, and is independent of all political pressure groups and commercial interests. It receives particular support from the Joseph Rowntree Memorial Trust.

The core of PSI's work is its wide-ranging programme of studies, organised and developed under six Research Groups responsible for a series of studies in the areas of the economy and the labour market, industrial development, politics and government, justice and social order, social policy and the quality of life.

The research methods include surveys, case studies, statistical analysis, literature and document search and discussion with practitioners and other researchers in seminars or groups.

A full list of PSI publications, and information about methods of ordering, are available from:

THE PUBLICATIONS DEPARTMENT
PSI, 100 Park Village East,
London NW1 3SR
Telephone: 01-387 2171

Copies of publications are displayed in PSI's reception at the above address, and are available for sale to individual purchasers.